Emotional Wholeness

Connecting With the Emotions of Jesus

Jane
Isa 9:6

Dick
2Tim I:24-26

D1416964

Emotional Wholeness

Connecting With the Emotions of Jesus

Dick and Jane Mohline

Treasure House

An Imprint of
Destiny Image® Publishers, Inc.
P.O. Box 310
Shippensburg, PA 17257-0310

"For where your treasure is,
there will your heart be also." Matthew 6:21

ISBN 1-56043-290-X

For Worldwide Distribution
Printed in the U.S.A.

This book and all other Destiny Image, Revival Press,
and Treasure House books are available
at Christian bookstores and distributors worldwide.

For a U.S. bookstore nearest you, call **1-800-722-6774**.
For more information on foreign distributors, call **717-532-3040**.
Or reach us on the Internet: **http://www.reapernet.com**

Endorsements

In *Emotional Wholeness*, Dick and Jane Mohline take the reader on a road seldom trod. Much has been written on the life of Jesus, but little attention has been given to His emotions and how He processed them. If Christ is our example in all of life, then certainly this includes our emotions. I predict that this book will spawn a rising interest in this often overlooked aspect of our Lord's life. It is a seedbed for reflection, for all who seek to understand and process human emotions.

Gary D. Chapman, Ph.D.
Senior Associate Pastor
Calvary Baptist Church

Reading this book can benefit you in three ways. First, you'll get to know Jesus and your Bible in a deeper way. Second, you'll better understand yourself and your emotions. Third, by putting what it teaches into practice, you'll discover how you and the Lord can work together to handle destructive emotions and difficult situations. I recommend this book highly. It's biblical, practical, and desperately needed in the Church today.

Warren W. Wiersbe
Author, Conference Speaker

Index of the Emotions of Jesus

Contents

Foreword

A Book of Distinction

Here is a book that is distinctive. It's refreshing to find a resource that is easily read and yet contains truths that open our eyes into the life of Jesus. Very few writers have attempted to take an honest look at the emotions of Jesus, but thankfully we now have a comprehensive overview.

Dick and Jane have explored the topic extensively, and the transitions from chapter to chapter keep the reader directly involved. There are insights and content in this volume not found elsewhere. As you read, you will be delighted by the practical applications this book gives for what we experience in our daily life. This resource will be beneficial to our understanding of our Lord, as well as help our Christian walk.

H. Norman Wright

Chapter One

Discovering and Connecting With the Emotions of Our Lord Jesus

For a child will be born to us,
a son will be given to us;
and the government will rest on His shoulders,
and His name will be called
Wonderful Counselor, Mighty God, Eternal Father,
Prince of Peace.

Isaiah 9:6

Our Wonderful Counselor and Prince of Peace truly was the God-man. He came to know all the diversities of life. Jesus loved and rejoiced. He knew gains, stresses, trials, angers, sufferings, joys, crises, dilemmas, losses, and temptations, while walking and moving through life. His wide range of emotions has been important to me for over 25 years. From Scripture I've discovered more than 30 of them. When God the Father, God the Son, and God the Holy Spirit created humanity, They designed us with these same healthy, appropriately expressed emotions. But in the Garden of Eden, Adam and Eve messed up the God-Head design with their sinful choices. They ignored the instructions of God to not eat from His "Knowledge Tree." (See Genesis 2:9,15-18; 3:1-6.) Their deliberate sin distorted the total personality of mankind, interfering with God's plan for our emotional wholeness. Humanity could no longer function in God's image. Having rejected God through Jesus Christ, the Perfect Personality, we then did and became what was right in our own eyes (see Judg. 17:6). Since then we have lived with a state of toxic emotions.

The Reality of Demonstrated Emotions From Christ and God

Until Christ came to earth, we had no **fit** model to follow for our personalities. Yet, He came into the world for such a time as this. Jesus became our model for the perfect personality. In addition, His death and resurrection provide within us the motivation to become a more fulfilled personality. Scripture says we "are being transformed into the same image...the image of the invisible God, the first-born of all creation" (2 Cor. 3:18; Col. 1:15). We do that by letting the same "mind be in [us], which was also in Christ Jesus" (Phil. 2:5 KJV). Yet, being transformed into His image is not only to "think" like Him but to *feel* like Him. Christ is more than a **thinker**; He is a *feeler*. Just as Jesus "increased...in favour with God and man" in His emotions, so can we (Lk. 2:52 KJV). Taking on His image includes conforming to His mind and will, plus connecting with His **emotions**. That's the way our "mind and emotions" come together.

Theologians and behavioral scientists alike have largely ignored the need for this "coming together." Consequently, for the most part they have not applied His wide range of healthy responses to their "life and walk" with Christ. Most either describe His emotions as completely different from ours or as having no difference at all. Looking at this fuzzy picture, it seems we either worship a detached and mechanical God-man or a reactive Man-god. Some even go so far to say that calling Christ the God-man helps create an "impossible combination." Those individuals fail to see Jesus as both fully human and fully Divine.

When we think about the God-man, should this unsolved puzzle surprise us? "No one has ever fully understood the nature of God; no one has ever fully known the nature of mankind...When we speak of the God-Man, we combine the greatest possible opposites—God and man united in one."[1] The union of His Deity and humanity, which some refer to as tensions of the hypostatic union, is of great importance in the area of Christ's person and nature. Because Christ's nature was sinless, His emotional expressions and responses were also completely pure. Discovering and connecting with His pure emotions is the only way to understand ourselves. This process moves us away from *toxic* emotions into emotional wholeness as our mind and emotions come together.

Overall, in studying Christ's life I've found that He felt more than love, compassion, and joy. His emotions I've discovered thus far include agony, amazed, anger, compassion, cried, deeply moved, depressed, fear, forsaken, fury, glad, grieved, hunger, indignation, joy, like, love, marveled, peace, pressure, rejoiced, sad, sighing deeply, sorrow, suffering, sympathy, shed tears, thirsty, troubled, weary, and wept.[2] There are different camps of thought, however, on His emotions. For example, some argue that "Jesus and feelings" depend on "God and feelings." They say that because God is spirit, He has no emotions. Yet, several Old Testament passages talk about different types of behavior He hates, like Proverbs 6:16-19. Scripture also talks about God's love for His Son and His created beings (see Jn. 3:16; 10:15-18; Gen. 1:26-27). Since God *hates* certain behavior and **loves** His Son and created beings, we can believe that He *feels* emotion. Besides His numerous healthy, appropriately expressed emotions, Christ speaks of a "oneness" and equal sharing between Him and God His Father with all things. These expressions demonstrate Their emotions.

Jesus Christ and His Environmental Influence

Some ask why Christ didn't let His emotional responses "fall out" onto others like we occasionally do. When Jesus was railed on, He railed not again; when Jesus suffered, He threatened not; deceit was not found in His mouth; Jesus did no sin, is the answer. His emotions never overmastered Him; He was always in control.[3] Yet, the God-man lived with environmental influence like all humanity has lived with. Although Christ had a Divine mind, He also had a human mind that functioned with a self-limited consciousness (see Phil. 2:5-8). Christ could be aware of only those things that He was conscious of at any given time in His surroundings. Jesus offered a stable and unchanging personality, while people and surroundings in His immediate world offered constant change with a varied environmental influence. When we put together the nature of Christ's character ingredients, His emotional expressions, and His environment, we see how He dealt with His surroundings.

Christ expressed His nature by relating to others with attachment, love, holiness, and joy. These are present in Him at all times and they never change. He expressed His many emotions one at a time; they were distinct and discernible. But the environmental influence offered a variety of challenges to Christ because it was in constant change. Adam and Eve, along with their family, provide a quick reminder of the emotional destructiveness that can come from an "always changing" environment. Their choices to ignore God and eat from the Knowledge Tree distorted the total personality of mankind. This toxic distortion spilled over onto the first two sons some time later when Cain expressed anger in an unhealthy, harmful way and killed Abel. This doing "what's right in his own eyes" added to the continual, changing environment.

Like Cain, each of us have built-in emotional responses based primarily on the toxic emotional responses modeled by parents or other significant adults. In my family, for example, the most prominent emotion was "rejection." This caused distant, cold relationships to develop between us. In Jane's family, "anger" was the most prominent emotion. That caused explosive relationships. Recognizing these background differences, seeking Scriptural models of Christ's emotions, and trying to apply them have helped us make significant adjustments in our relational conflicts. These choices help us separate our toxic emotions from the environmental influence. This is only one example of why we need to discover and connect with Christ's stable, practical models for healthy emotional responses.

Connecting With the Emotions of Jesus

While defining *emotions* is not easy, we could "see" them as a basic motivational force that affects feelings, thoughts, and responses. We express these through body movements, facial expressions, and vocal tones.[4] In fact, Jesus says to love the Lord with all our heart, soul, strength, and mind (see Mk. 12:30). This is another way to bring mind and emotions together. Since emotional responses vary in degree and intensity, our up-and-down emotions influence all areas of work, learning, relationships, and worship. We can greatly encourage each other by believing that each of us may be affected in different ways by the same emotion. We can believe also that the depth of life's situations, whether sad or happy, greatly influences our emotions.

Next, we need to think about how our emotional responses help show personal characteristics. For instance, some of us are known for an easy smile while others are known for a frozen frown. Looking behind Christ's emotional expressions to the character from which His responses came is helpful. Some point out that Scripture does not describe Christ as laughing or smiling. At the same time, though, I point to His joy and compassion, which surely affected many facial and emotional responses.[5] On the other hand, many confuse smiling from the **heart** with smiling from a plastic facial expression. These plastic smiles hide our raw and toxic emotions, damaged by the depth of life's situations. In covering the whole range of Christ's emotions, I haven't found one verse to indicate that He at any time felt mixed feelings about His emotions. He didn't need to repress any emotion; His many different emotions were never in conflict.

Scripture reveals a wide variety of emotions and responses from Jesus. Although the face mirrors most of our emotions, there is only one reference to Christ's facial expressions (see Lk. 9:51). This does not mean that He lived without enthusiasm. There are only two physiological references that talk about Christ shedding tears and sweating like drops of blood from ruptured capillaries, as He prayed (see Lk. 22:44; Heb. 5:7). These responses show that He lived with intensity, concern, and energy. When we look at examples of Jesus speaking about His emotional state together with His social situations, we gain further insight about His emotions and responses (see Mt. 15:32; 26:37).

Jesus models personality through His emotions, relationships, mind, self-image, and will. But in the following chapters we will focus only on His **emotions**. At times the Scriptural understanding of Christ's emotions Jane and I present may seem to conflict with your views. If this happens, I ask you to spend a few minutes thinking about whether the view is relevant. But my overall hope is that you will still find Scripture presented as relevant for your own needs. As you connect with the healthy, appropriate emotions of Jesus, may your mind and emotions come together so you can experience emotional wholeness.

Chapter Two

Jesus Felt Inner Peace
While
Walking Through Life

Peace I leave with you;
My peace I give to you;
not as the world gives, do I give to you.
Let not your heart be troubled,
nor let it be fearful.

John 14:27

"Those who do not love Me do not obey My teaching, the Word that comes from My Father" (Jn. 14:24 par.). Jesus was answering questions from His disciples. He explained that He doesn't disclose Himself to the world because those who **don't** love or believe in Him do not keep His Word. On the flip side, those who **do** love Him and keep His Commandments will receive a blessing of triple portions. One portion is the love of Jesus and His Father. The second, is Jesus making Himself known to us. The third, is Jesus and God making Their home within us through the Holy Spirit. The Holy Spirit comes from the Father in Jesus' name to teach and help us learn. He will bring to remembrance all things Jesus taught while He lived, worked, and fellowshiped with His disciples. That's why Jesus can disclose Himself only to those who believe in Him. This disclosure shows us that He's in the Father, that we are in Him, and that He is in us to give peace. His peace, though, is not like what the world offers. We can not work for it; it's ours free to receive through the Holy Spirit.[1] His peace doesn't consist of freedom from turmoil or suffering; it's a calm undeviating devotion to God's will.[2]

Times of Feeling Inward Peace on Earth

Emotions we all have. But we don't always know what to do with our emotions and responses. For many years I have counseled with men and women from different ages and backgrounds. These people bring a variety of emotional needs, as they look for peace. Of course, there's only one true peace; that is the peace Jesus gives through the Holy Spirit.[3] Jesus Christ's peace comes first of all from experiencing personal forgiveness of sin through faith in His death, burial, and resurrection. His peace provides a tranquil state for each of us who is assured of salvation through faith in Christ, who helps us with our fears. Christ assured His disciples that His peace is different from that of the world where the normal experience is trial, tribulation, distress, disappointment, and frustration. His peace will cut through those heavy experiences to give us His inner tranquility in their midst.

The Reality of Inward Peace

The God-man knows explicitly about this world system and what it has to offer. He helped create lucifer, the most beautiful of creatures, and later witnessed him fall from heaven like lightning. Sometime later Jesus suffered severe temptation from the devil, yet not once did He give in to sin. Jesus enjoyed His inner tranquility at all times. Yet, Scripture says clearly those who follow the devil have no inner tranquility in mind, conscience, or heart. That's because they are engaged continually in active hostility against God.[4] When we follow Christ, His inner tranquility is ours even when attacked by the devil's evil world system. Christ gives His peace to us in order to meet our innermost needs because He doesn't want our hearts to feel troubled or fearful. His *peace* is the peace "which passeth all understanding" (Phil. 4:7 KJV). Jesus left this peace for each of us to keep our emotions from being taken hostage. When we receive and apply His inner peace, He strengthens and stabilizes us while walking through life.

My mother-in-law explained once about times of inward peace for her. Mother Allen gave birth to ten babies, each was born at home. For several births, she had only a midwife to help her because the country doctor could not arrive in time. Mom said that with each birth she waited anxiously to hold her baby for the first time. She would lovingly hold and talk with the baby as she looked into its eyes. When she saw the baby's beautiful, clear eyes—which signified to her there were no brain deficiencies—a feeling of *peace* would flood her emotions. Through that inner tranquility she gave thanks to the Lord for her healthy baby. Memories of physical pain or suffering felt during the birth were released and removed by her inward peace.

Many portray our emotions as being in conflict with our *spiritual* side. Rather than healthy motivators, they are perceived as mere expressions of the *flesh*. When we believe such teachings, we often deny our emotions in order to try to contain and control them. Our rigid, controlled feelings then take precedence over understanding how emotions are really reflections of an inner character. This can cause a split in our personalities. Yet, Jesus Christ did not have or model a split personality. He did not mask or pretend or plasticize His feelings. His emotional responses were in complete agreement with His thoughts and feelings. As God-man, Jesus felt no conflict between flesh or spirit or emotions. He felt inward peace.

One Example of Finding Inward Peace

Since Christ has overcome the world, we who believe in and follow Him have access to His peaceful inner tranquility and harmony. But for the first 20 years of my life, I felt no inward peace. Although my parents were Christians, they failed to build closeness in their relationship. As a result, they did not develop a close emotional attachment with me or my siblings. Lacking closeness with them, I looked elsewhere; consequently, friends became most important to me. Wanting approval, I learned to please others. When visiting friends, they would encourage me to join them in drinking from their parents' beverage bars. Drinking alcohol made me feel accepted and important, even as a preteen.

Ironically, the church my family attended believed children should be baptized at age 12. On a particular Sunday, 12-year-olds were lined up at the altar and asked, "Do you believe in Jesus Christ?" On my Sunday by the time they reached me I knew the correct answer was, "Yes." So, I was baptized and joined the church; sadly, though, my heart had not been changed.

My drinking, an emotional security blanket, led to lying and gambling, affecting my student life. I began skipping school to drink, smoke, and play cards with my buddies. My parents were called to the principal's office many times because of my absences and low grades. One day, with Mother and Dad at work, my buddies gathered in our dining room. In the middle of a "hand" we noticed a police car pull up. To avoid being caught, all of them went flying out windows and the back door. Their school books, left behind, provided names for the policemen to give to school authorities. Lacking motivation or discipline to study, I had to repeat my junior year; after that, I was told to not come back for my senior year. By age 18, I suffered from ulcers because of alcohol abuse. No one held the key to my toxic emotions and need for inward peace.

About two years later, my father's work moved him to Chicago, Illinois. The only place where my parents could find a house to rent was the suburb college-town of Wheaton. Because of my bad influence on the younger children, they asked me to stay in the East. Later, I moved to Wheaton and found a construction job working with a group of Christians. They witnessed to me through their everyday life. One night they invited me to attend evangelistic meetings at Wheaton College held by Dr. Stephen Olford from England. That night I heard the gospel of Jesus Christ for my first time. In learning that it was for me He died, my heart was stirred. I felt too uncomfortable to walk forward in front of all those people, so I rushed home. In my room, I knelt and prayed. "God, I don't know how to pray. But if what the man talked about is true, I want that." God heard and answered that prayer.

Christ saw my sinful, empty heart and filled it with His forgiveness, cleansing, and love and filled my soul with the Holy Spirit. He met my spiritual need for inner peace and began healing my toxic emotions. Next day, I flushed my cigarettes down the toilet and other unneeded, unhealthy habits began dropping off. God led "Skip" to help me. He was from the Navigators, an organization started by Dawson Trotman to disciple Christians in studying and memorizing Scripture. Getting God's truth into my mind started changing my thinking and my feelings.

Soon after this, the Lord led me to attend Wheaton Academy where I finished my high school education. As Christ renewed my mind and emotions, He empowered me to study, concentrate, memorize, learn, work, and develop healthy friendships. After graduating, He led me to the Moody Bible Institute, Wheaton College, and Gordon Seminary for further training and grounding in Scripture. Later at Loyola University, I finished the schooling process necessary for God's calling on my life. Yet, praise His name, when I was distressed and downcast like sheep without a shepherd Jesus saw me in the multitudes and met my need for salvation and inward peace.

Jesus and Feeling Inward Peace

Scripture does not explicitly say Jesus felt peace. Yet we can say He "felt peace" since He is the Lord and King of peace. John records Jesus saying, "My peace I give to you" (Jn. 14:27). This inner peace came from an untroubled, unfearful heart in the midst of suffering and conflict. Jesus can give peace because He *feels* peace; His peace carries free access to God.[5] Yet, Christ's peace is not passive. Nor is it like that of the evil world system, which offers counterfeits then takes them back after we are hooked. Christ's peace involves our thought life and learning to take every thought captive to Him (see 2 Cor. 10:5). This speaks of commitment and hard work. When we allow lies, evil suggestions, envy, doubt, or the like to "stay" in our thoughts, peace is destroyed. In order for Christ's peace to "keep our hearts and minds," our thoughtlife must continually be placed under His control to patrol "the issues of life."

The inner peace of Jesus is not an absence of problems nor did He live without problems. It's next to impossible for us to continually receive Christ's peace when we unconsciously place His responses to life on the same level as ours. We must see Him as one vastly different from us, with eternal excellence. Christ did not feel upheaval or unrest in His inner man; rather, He enjoyed emotional calmness.[6] How fitting then that He encourages us followers to not allow our hearts to feel fearful or troubled. Jesus offers us His inner tranquility and harmony for decision making, loving others, and obeying our Holy Father. His peace within us can truly calm and settle our fearful, troubled hearts; it's ours to feel, enjoy, and keep. One secret of that peace was His certainty in knowing that "the prince of this world cometh, and hath nothing in Me" (Jn. 14:30 KJV). This strong assurance from Jesus about His sinlessness, gives us peace. Shortly, our Lord and Savior shall bruise satan under our feet. That encourages us also to have nothing to do with the devil. It's our responsibility through acceptance, obedience, and submission to choose Christ's practical pattern for our inner peace.

First, we can experience Christ's peace through accepting Jesus as our Savior through personal faith in Him. Through salvation we receive Jesus' peace that He left for and gives to His followers.

Second, we can experience Christ's peace through our obedience to Him. Jesus called us to peace; through obedience to Him, He is allowed to be our peace.

Third, we can experience Christ's peace through submitting to Him. We choose to *let* His "soul harmony" rule our hearts in all situations by submitting to His will and standards for our lives.[7]

Summarizing Our Thoughts on Jesus and Life and Inward Peace

Once, when teaching Scripture to the Philippians, Paul asked, "Now that I have taught you these truths, what then?" or "So what?" During my seminary studies, I also learned that we can profit by asking that question. "So what?" So what that Jesus is willing to give His inner peace to us followers? What can that do for you? First, if you aren't sure of your salvation, talk to a trusted Christian (or call Jane or I) who can show you from Scripture how to believe in Christ. Study Scripture pertaining to attitudes, schedules, and choices. As the Holy Spirit teaches you from Scripture, begin to submit to Christ. You must use Christ's pattern to feel His inner peace. In the next chapter we will discover why Christ had a healthy fear for God's authority while He walked through life.

Chapter Three

Jesus Felt a Healthy Fear for God's Authority While
Walking Through Life

In the days of His flesh
[Jesus] offered up definite, special petitions...
and supplications, with strong crying and tears,
to Him Who was [always] able to save Him (out) from death,
and He was heard because of His reverence toward God
—His godly fear....

Hebrews 5:7 AMP

"You are My Son, today I have begotten You" (Heb. 5:5 AMP). Never has there been a high priest like Jesus, the Son of God. As the God-man, He had the two qualifications necessary for fulfilling the role of a valid priesthood. His humanity provided sympathy and His Deity provided strength. A high priest had to be chosen; he could not place himself in that position. A priest was to act for mankind in things pertaining to God. He must offer both gifts and sacrifices for the sins of mankind, as well as for his own. Jesus, who had no personal ambition for the position, was appointed a priest forever by God His Father after the order of Melchizedek. As our sinless High Priest, He had no need to sacrifice on His behalf. Jesus gave Himself once as a blood sacrifice for your and my sin. But before that, He brought to God the offering of "a heart torn with anguish and suffering, a soul in which the conflict of the ages was raging."[1] Jesus gave this offering of strong crying and tears as He walked along in a trusting caution about what lay ahead.[2] The Father **heard** and answered Jesus' petition because of His reverent, trusting, godly fear for God's sovereign authority.[3]

Feeling a Healthy Fear for God's Authority

Respect for and submission to God's authority have nearly ceased to function in this "cult of self" society. Almost from birth, society teaches our children that **self** is #1 in importance. Manipulating others for the good of self has become a favorite pastime, encouraging an ongoing fascination with a "me generation." It's as though *self* has become a product-of-the-year for which we seek diligently to promote. In so doing, we have created a crisis that's about to erupt.

> "[This] crisis is in the character of our culture, where the values that restrain inner vices and develop inner virtues are eroding. Unprincipled men and women, disdainful of their moral heritage and skeptical of Truth itself, are destroying our civilization by weakening the very pillars upon which it rests."[4]

Overindulgence with "self" has opened a floodgate freeing obsessive fears that are drowning us. You and I feel fear several times each day, whether or not we will admit to this. Fear is used more times in Scripture than the word "love." Since fear masquerades under different names, we don't always recognize it or know what to do with the feeling. Timidity causes us to act cowardly.[5] Jesus never at any time acted as a coward. Terror causes us to feel tormented and in bondage.[6] Although the devil tried many times to subject Jesus to terror, He did not at any time feel in bondage or tormented. Some have identified at least 26 phobias lurking in the dark and hanging around each emotional corner. These unhealthy, out-of-proportion fears range from achlophobia (fear of crowds) to zoophobia (fear of animals).[7] On the flip side, Jesus modeled a reverential and godly fear for His Holy Father.[8] This balanced, healthy feeling you and I can also develop in our lives toward God's authority. Developing that balance will help release us from ugly, obsessive *fears* caused by living for self.

The Reality of Unhealthy Fear Toward God's Authority

For years we have been told that within us lives a wonderful, beautiful personality, waiting to burst out. We're assured that this amazing personality will blossom into splendor if we will just forget God's authority, common courtesy, and cooperating with others. These "choices" will free us to proceed to do exactly what we "feel" like doing. This high ranking attitude called *cult of self*, replaces *agape* love and compassion for others. Can we wonder, then, that a reverential fear for God's authority has flown out the window? We now see that in spite of an untiring, unlimited indulgence and uninhibited passion in society, "the cult of *self* has left thousands dissatisfied."[9] The Cinderella myth of living for self doesn't work. We cannot develop a healthy trust for God's authority when enthralled with *self*.

In society we find only two kinds of people. One kind says to **God**, "Thy will be done." The other kind says to **self**, "*Thy* will be done."[10] Anyone living for self soon discovers that self-discovery leading to life satisfaction does not come from overindulgence and uninhibited passion. The only basis for lasting and satisfying self-discovery rests on understanding and accepting the fact that we are created in God's image with mind, soul, and emotions. (See Genesis 1:26-27.) From there we further enrich our lives by developing self-identity through Christ-designed choices for salvation and personhood. From there we move to a Christ-designed work for ministry and livelihood. At the same time, we need a Christ-designed commitment in relationships. Christ's design for self-discovery is the only way to dethrone "me first" behavior and experience healthy self-satisfaction. Christ's design will also help free us to develop an inner **healthy** reverential fear for God's sovereign authority rather than living for self.

One Example of Living for Self and Not Revering God

Concentrating on self binds us, narrows us, limits us, and keeps us from following Christ's model in revering God. A biblical example of one enthralled with an oppressive cult of self is Esau, twin brother to Jacob, whose parents were Isaac and Rebekah. Jacob developed into a plain, quiet man who dwelt in tents; to the opposite, Esau developed into a cunning hunter enjoying the outdoors. One might think that outdoors men would develop endurance, stamina, and emotional control. But from living for self, Esau failed to develop self-control; he thought only of what he wanted, and when he wanted it. Consequently, Esau did not possess the inner strength that comes from self-control. He demanded immediate attention from anyone he could con into serving him.

Coming home from hunting one day, Esau felt hungry and wanted instant food gratification. He smelled a stew that Jacob had fixed for lunch and loudly demanded, "Give me some of that red lentil stew, for I'm starved!" Jacob, the manipulator, had learned well how to get what he wanted by underhanded means. So he responded, "I will, if you will sell me your rights of a firstborn son right now." Having spent his life living for instant gratification, Esau had no inner reserve on which to call.

Merely feeling hunger pangs from missing one meal made him think he was surely dying. When Jacob insisted that he sell him his birthright that day, Esau did so on the spot. Uninhibited passion and overindulgence had weakened Esau to the point of "scorning" a birthright that entitled him to inherit all his parents' possessions, just for a serving of bread and stew. (See Genesis 25:19-34.)

Esau developed no inner emotional control or reserve and lived only for self. To the opposite, Jacob's jealousy kept him from developing an ability to consider others' weaknesses. Furthermore, Jacob wanted so badly to have something that belonged to Esau that he refused to back off. He took advantage of Esau in his weakness. Both brothers learned dysfunctional relationships from parents who were, also, steeped in dysfunctional living. Scripture says that Isaac was partial to Esau and Rebekah was partial to Jacob (see Gen. 25:28). This is one way generational curses can come into being and then passed on until broken through spiritual-warfare prayer. Our Holy Father said, "I the Lord your God am a jealous God, visiting the iniquity of the fathers upon the children to the third and fourth generation..." (Ex. 20:5 AMP). Isaac and Rebekah passed on a "cult of self" to Jacob and Esau which they had learned from Abraham and Sarah, their parents. Neither family had admitted a destructive lifestyle of selfish control and prideful codependency. For three generations, we see no clear expression of a healthy fear for God's authority in their relationships.

Jesus Christ and God's Authority and Healthy Fear

In all of Christ's life on earth we see that He expressed a healthy, reverential fear for God's sovereign authority. His fear, however, was not terror, not cowardliness, and not a dread of God. Instead, Christ felt a healthy reverence for His Father. This helped Him obey God's sovereign authority and He willingly stepped into it by saying, "Lo, I come...to do Thy will, O God" (Heb. 10:7 KJV). Jesus acknowledged and respected God's authority in many different ways. One way was in admitting that since the Father begat Him, the Father is greater than He. Christ revealed that He could do nothing independently of the Father, that the Father sent Him to earth. Under God's authority and directions, Jesus received commandments. Furthermore, the Holy Father gave Jesus His own authority and the message He declared on earth. The Father accomplished works through Him. Jesus received His Kingdom from the Father and will ultimately deliver it back to Him.

The Father did not "hear" Jesus merely because He was the only begotten, sinless Son. God heard and answered Jesus because of His godly fear and reverential trust for the Father. Because of their trust-based relationship, Christ was free to be vulnerable with His Heavenly Parent. He unashamedly came to God with a heart filled with agony as He faced the powers of darkness, waging a battle for our sin. *Trust*, not terror or cowardliness, brought forth prayers washed with strong crying and tears as Jesus submitted with a trusting caution of what lay ahead. This gave Him an audience with God. Like God the Father is head of Christ, Christ is the head of His Church. We come to God for salvation by way of faith in Christ because Jesus submits to the Father's sovereign authority. He respected, trusted, and obeyed God's authority.[11] His behavior shows us how we also can revere God and His authority while walking through life.

First, Jesus submitted Himself to God's authority. He did not seek position or status or power; He accepted God's design for His life on earth.

Second, Jesus openly expressed His emotional responses to the Father. He did not deny feelings, or hesitate, or withdraw from Their relationship. In strong crying and shedding tears Jesus talked with the Father when He felt the need.

Third, Jesus trusted God's sovereignty and wisdom. He received responsibility, power, and glory from God to help Him do the Father's will.[12] Christ's straightforward, practical model is possible for each of us to follow.

Summarizing Our Thoughts on Jesus and God's Authority and Healthy Fear

"So what?" So what that Jesus felt a healthy fear for God's authority while walking through life? What does this do for you? Have you swallowed some of the New Age belief that we're little gods and can live life by our own power? Do you struggle with how to feel a reverential trust for God? Like Jesus did, submit yourself to God's authority. Don't seek position or status or power, let God choose those for you; accept His design for your life on earth. Like Jesus did, express your emotional responses openly to the Father. You need not deny feelings, or hesitate, or withdraw from your relationship with God. If you feel the need, talk to the Father with crying and shedding of tears. Like Jesus did, trust God's sovereignty and wisdom. Receive from Him responsibility, power, and glory to help you do His will. But remember that it's your responsibility to connect with

Jesus' emotional response model. Otherwise, He can't bless and help you develop a healthy fear for trusting God's authority as you walk through life. In the next chapter we will discover why Jesus felt pressure in dealing with stress.

Chapter Four

Jesus Felt Pressure
in
Dealing With Stress

But I have a baptism to undergo,
and how pressured I am
until it is accomplished!

Luke 12:50 ILT

"Someone did touch Me, for I was aware that power had gone out of Me" (Lk. 8:46). A woman suffering for 12 years from blood hemorrhage wanted to be healed. She maneuvered her way through the crowd to those surrounding Jesus. While He was not looking, this woman timidly reached out and touched the bottom edge of His cloak. Immediately, her bleeding stopped. Jesus, being very sensitive to any healing power leaving His body, liked to meet those who came to touch Him. He liked to hear them tell of His touch on their lives and enjoyed talking with them. Many had touched Jesus for healing, so the disciples were amazed that He asked for such detail. "Master, the people crowd and press You and You ask us who touched You? How can we possibly know?" The healed woman, hearing their conversation, wondered if she had done wrong. Not understanding why Jesus wanted to know, she fearfully came forward and identified herself. After the healed woman explained why she had needed His touch, Jesus praised her for exercising faith in the face of a most difficult situation.[1] Jesus sent the woman on her way in peace. But in dealing with the healings and the large crowd, He had felt pressured.[2]

The Stress of Handling Life's Pressure Points

Pressure points are common to each of us. Their sharp points prick us daily as we walk through life. Since we differ in personalities, come from various backgrounds, and live with a multitude of daily decisions, our pressure points are not the same. So it was with Christ. That woman with a blood hemorrhage was in the midst of a multitude of people waiting for Him as He walked into Galilee from the country of Gerasenes. But Jairus, a synagogue official, immediately approached Christ, begging Him to come and heal his 12-year-old daughter. At his house, a crowd laughed at the idea of Jesus healing the child. Pressure points. Jesus had the complex problem of trying to deal with both friendly and hostile crowds. He felt crowded and pressed outwardly as well as inwardly. Wherever Christ went, He had to cope with pressure points.

The Reality of Stress in Pressure

Although all pressure we feel in trying to handle life's pressure points is not bad, it can cause us emotional stress. When experiences cause us to be in a state of mental restraint where we feel hard-pressed by the urgency of circumstances, that's pressure.[3] Jesus felt this type of stressful pressure when thinking about the urgency of dying for your and my sin (see Lk. 12:50). Another type of pressure comes when we are pressed on all sides and feel squeezed emotionally, while trying to deal with others' demands. In trying to deal with the healings and crowds, Christ felt the weight of being pressed and squeezed emotionally (see Lk. 8:45). Even though there are three other Greek words for *pressure* in the New Testament, only those two are used to describe Christ.[4] One important difference to remember about the reality of stress is that while Christ *felt* pressured and squeezed, He was not the source of His stress. His dealing with either friendly or hostile crowds plus anticipating death on a cross for your and my sin provided the source of Christ's inward and outward pressure points.

One Example of Pressure Points

Recognizing my pressure points is not easy. My tendency is to keep going, keep trying, keep smiling, and keep ignoring. As a result, I can overload my schedule and make too many commitments without being aware of my overcrowded circumstances. The overload, however, does not stop at the office. Overload carries over to my home. Jane, who is very sensitive to schedule balance, begins to feel neglected when my mental, emotional, and energy levels near depletion. When I overload, much to her displeasure, she finds herself once again having to blow the "stop whistle" and uncover my overcrowded circumstances. For both of us, this becomes a stressful pressure point.

Since I'm now working half-time for two separate organizations in two different states, overcrowding of schedules easily happens. Counseling with clients, helping administrate our large church in the senior pastor's absence, and flying to meetings don't leave much time for my commitment to Jane or family or friends. Especially, since it is difficult for my mouth to say "No" to opportunities. These experiences often create in me a state of mental restraint, and I feel hard-pressed by the urgency of my circumstances. When Jane has to blow the "stop whistle" I feel the *ol' squeeze* of being pressed on all sides. It's apparent that I sometimes forget to follow Christ's model of coping with life's pressure points.

The Results of Stressful Pressure Points

Feeling pressure points is one thing, but failure to deal with them is quite another. Stress that's not dealt with can "create upset stomachs, gnawing fear, splitting headaches, intense grief, excessive drinking, and violent arguments."[5] When our pressure points cause ongoing stress, they must be dealt with for our health's sake. Are you aware of your pressure points? Are they from your behavior and decision making, or are others the source of that emotional pressure? LouAnn, like other incest survivors who have not dealt with their emotional damage, is often the cause of her pressures. Since her feelings of self-esteem are so damaged, she seeks others' approval through unwise and unhealthy choices. Because LouAnn "allows" others to take advantage of her, she lives with a low-grade, unresolved anger. Under pressure from unpaid bills, a broken car, and a disliked job, she sometimes spews her anger onto the innocent. This will cause problems for them as well as for her.

Stress not dealt with can affect us like a scuba diver who doesn't have sufficient air pressure. A scuba diver gets in trouble fast if his air-pressure tank isn't adjusted properly, enabling him to dive down or come up quickly. Air pressure inside his suit must be as great as the water pressure pressing on the outside; otherwise, severe stomach cramps will hit. Likewise, in order for us to be able to deal with emotional pressures, our "inside pressures" must equal our "outside pressures." Jesus Christ, living within us through the Holy Spirit, provides our needed inner-pressure strength. But we must receive and use His provision. Since LouAnn is not using His provision, she has not given up unhealthy and unwise decisions. Therefore, she is kept from competent information and needed guidance for personal growth, and caves in under pressure. The inside spiritual pressure she needs for strength is not equal to her outside life pressure points.

Christ and Pressure Points

Christ lived with many pressure points in each phase of His life here on earth. Even as a baby and toddler, life was stressful since Mary and Joseph had to protect Him from King Herod's jealous, vicious attempts to end His young life. Going into His teen years, knowing He would have to wait 12 more years before "being about His Father's business" was a pressure point. Later, as an adult, Jesus was not immune to pressure when He felt hard-pressed by the urgency of life circumstances. Once His three-year ministry started, everywhere Jesus went the people followed, "crowding and pressing upon Him." Speaking of the cross, Christ told His disciples that **He** had a baptism to pass under, and felt pressured until it would be accomplished.[6] Thinking about all that goes with dying on a cross gave Christ feelings of stressful urgency.

When dealing with personalities, healings, and large crowds, Christ felt squeezed and pressed outwardly as well as inwardly. Yet, He was not the *source* of His stress. Neither did feeling pressured and squeezed by stressful circumstances defeat Jesus. He gave us a practical and realistic model from the above experiences for dealing with life's pressure points.

First, Christ stayed sensitive to His emotional responses and physical strength. But He kept a balance of time, emotions, mind, and energy. He did not overcommit, overload, or overcrowd His schedule.

Second, Christ stayed sensitive to others by focusing on their overall needs. Moreover, in healing sicknesses and weaknesses, He kept a balance and did not deplete His physical and emotional reserves.

Third, Christ stayed sensitive to His commitment of doing God's will. He kept a balance between will and emotions, never losing sight at any time of why He came to live on earth.[7] Because Christ dealt with stress instead of denying it, His inner strength equaled His outside pressures. That's why He can understand our stressful pressure points in everyday life.

Summarizing Our Thoughts on Jesus and Stress and Pressure

"So what?" So what that Jesus felt pressure in dealing with stress? What does this do for you? Do you struggle unsuccessfully with stressful circumstances? Are you sometimes the source of that stress? Like Christ, stay sensitive to your emotional responses and physical strength by keeping a balance in your time, emotions, mind, and energy. Like Christ, refuse to overcommit, overload, or overcrowd your life and guard against depleting your physical and emotional reserves. Like Christ, stay sensitive to doing God's will but keep a balance between your will and emotions. Remember that it's your responsibility to accept the challenge to discover and connect with Jesus' emotions. Otherwise, His model cannot help you in dealing with the stress of pressure. In the next chapter, we will discover how Christ dealt with the stress of agony.

Chapter Five

Jesus Felt Agony
in
Dealing With Stress

And being in agony
He was praying very fervently;
and His sweat became like drops of blood,
falling down upon the ground.

Luke 22:44

"Father, if Thou art willing, remove this cup from Me; yet not My will, but Thine be done" (Lk. 22:42). Time was almost gone. Sounds from the soldiers' heavy, high-laced, hobnailed boots signaled that they were coming to take Christ away. Jesus was on His knees in the Garden of Gethsemane, crying out to God in agonizing, fervent prayer. Realizing that His time to die on a cross had come, He was agonizing over the conflict of obeying and doing the Father's will. Yet, the pain in His mind had not come so much from thoughts of dying as much as from stressful agonizing over submitting His human will to the Father's will. This opposition of the God-man's human will to God's Divine will had deepened the depth and severity of His agony over that decision, causing His capillaries to rupture. Sweat dribbling down His forehead became like drops of blood. Christ chose to do the Father's will and put Himself through the humiliation of death on a cross, although He knew that meant suffering excruciating pain. Obeying the Holy Father's will meant that Jesus would "be made" sin, for your and my sin. That would be His ultimate agony.[1]

The Stress of Agonizing Over Decisions

When we suffer severe mental struggles and emotions, we're in a battleground conflict of agony.[2] Being in a state of agony, even over decisions, feels like the armpit of life. While growing into adulthood, we learned to evaluate and test reality by decisions. Sadly, many of us moved into adult decision time without having had a "guided" trial-and-error learning. We didn't have mature parents or teachers to teach us soundness in making decisions based on the "sowing and reaping" principle. Some parents are so overprotective and fearful of their children making mistakes, they won't let them make even small decisions. Therefore, their children grow up without the needed confidence for making decisions, having learned to fear making choices and reaping the results. On the flip side, there are parents who don't want the responsibility of "guiding" their children through the trial-and-error years. They abdicate their parental role by allowing the children, even toddlers, to do whatever, whenever, wherever. Those children do not learn how to "count the cost" with choices, and therefore make them too lightly. From not having a childhood with "guided" decision making, whether too rigid or too loose, adulthood choices often cause us stress.

The Reality of Stress in Agony

One common understanding of stress says it's "essentially the wear and tear of living." Stress has even been called "the virus of our era."[3] Jesus felt the wear and tear of living just like you and I do. Because the virus of rampant sin covers our society, there are even more decisions today wearing and tearing our emotions. For those of us who tend to deny this, we feel the affects of stress without realizing what's happening. In recent years we have discovered how ongoing stress not dealt with damages our health. To clearly define stress is difficult; however, we can see and feel its effects. We are told that, "Stress dulls our memories, cripples our thinking, weakens our bodies, upsets our plans, stirs up our emotions, and reduces our efficiency."[4] Even when we believe the blurry teaching that God protects us from everyday trauma, we still will feel those stressful effects on our bodies and emotional systems.

That helps us understand why ongoing stress not dealt with is one of the main reasons we "lose" many fine pastors, missionaries, and other Christian workers. They become addicted to busyness and rescuing others; as a result, they can't stop for family time and needed rest. "Without realizing it, we have adopted the pace and standard of the world, and somehow we expect to escape the price that the world is paying—fractured marriages, nervous breakdowns, emotional burnout, and various degrees of depression and inability to cope."[5] When Christians fail to take care of their bodies—the Holy Spirit's temple, we "reap what we sow." The failure to relax, rest, eat nutritious food, and take vitamins and minerals, can actually offset our Bible study and prayer time. Stress not dealt with can deplete our inner emotional and physical reserves, causing agony for us Christians as well as for unbelievers.

The Stress Connected With Agony

Have you ever experienced doing God's will as stressful and filled with agony? There are times when Jane and I find that doing God's will can result in stressful mental and emotional struggle. Paul also found this to be true. He felt the type of agony that is called intense anxiety.[6] Paul felt very anxious when he tried to encourage the Philippi Christians as they faced suffering and opposition for Christ's sake. Paul felt intensely anxious as he tried to convince Christians that God had given them boldness so they could speak the gospel amidst much opposition. Another time, when he exhorted Timothy to flee earthly desires and run to heavenly virtues, he felt anxiety. And when Paul endured and persevered in preaching the gospel, that was anxiety-producing for him.[7] The fact that Paul tried to cope with stressful, agonizing circumstances can be helpful and encouraging to us.

After teaching little children for 30 years, Anne began to notice deterioration in her health. Ulcers and inability to cope with the smallest problems signaled a turning point for her. She went through several different types of medical exams. The overall evaluation said she needed time off work in order for inner healing to begin. She was suffering from the type of agony where we contend with adversaries and struggle with strenuous zeal over stressful circumstances.[8] She had to see different doctors and a counselor regularly. Some days felt less stressful than others; during those days it was easier for Anne to believe God was intervening. But during the more stressful days it was easier to doubt and feel that God had forgotten about her. Yet throughout her time of healing, Anne kept going to Scripture for encouragement and strength. From her interdependence with the Lord, He enabled her to experience a year of recovery and healing before returning to the classroom and a rewarding, successful career.

When God sees we're serious about doing His will, He sends the help that's best for us. The **help** may not always be that for which we want or hope. In the overall picture, though, we can feel confident with King David that "God's way is blameless" as He teaches us His ways (see Ps. 18:30). Anne agrees that even when we pass through agonizing times, like Christ did, learning God's ways through faith in Christ is best.

One Example of Agonizing Over Stressful Decision Making

Most of us, like Christ, experience some degree of agony in decision making. Regardless of our position and responsibilities, times of agonizing over decisions can cause stress. Trying to please someone, or determining God's will, or developing healthy thoughts rather than dwelling on evil, are just a few examples of how we sometimes agonize during decision time. Jane and I sometimes hold seminars on handling stress. Although we usually try to practice what we teach, we don't live without stressful decisions. About two years ago, we had to choose between two very stressful situations. For five years we had talked and prayed about where to move when I finished my ministry at the Rosemead School of Psychology in southern California. I was one year away from my 65th birthday, and Rosemead was starting its 25th year of service.[9] Leaving at that crucial time did not seem the right time. Jane, however, had finished a degree program and didn't believe she could find meaningful employment for only one year. We discovered in a new way that obedience to God's will can involve agonizing.

Three of our four adult children lived in the Midwest and East, and originally we had come from there. So we decided the best decision was to move closer to most of our children and families. We agreed that if God provided funds necessary for us to buy a house where our "original roots" had been, Jane would move there while I would stay in California one more year. God opened a door, so we walked through it by moving Jane with most of our furniture and belongings to Arkansas.

Although we knew only two people in Siloam Springs, the house we bought sits by a house owned by Marie, an 83-year-old Christian woman. She became a good friend to Jane. God led us to a vibrant, lively church where I now serve as Associate Pastoral Counselor. I couldn't visit with Jane more than once a month; however, an 800 telephone number enabled us to talk briefly each evening. While Jane remodeled some of our 50-year-old house, I phased out many years of counseling, teaching, and administrating at Rosemead. During that year, there were many very stressful situations and decisions with which we had to cope. At the same time, God provided for us, guided us, and gave us strength.

Jesus Christ and Stressful Decisions and Agony

Christ did not live without stress. He lived with the "wear and tear of living."[10] We can *sense* the tightening of His nerves and muscles as He struggled in a battleground conflict in prayer. At the end, when He surrendered

His human will to God's Divine will, an angel from Heaven came and strengthened Him. Later, Christ walked over to where He thought His disciples would be praying for Him. They were there, but they were asleep. The most agonizing night of Jesus' life as He struggled between two irreconcilable wills, His and God's, His disciples slept rather than stand with Him in the prayer gap. That sight aggravated His already severe and extreme mental anguish.

Agonizing over stressful decisions and handling life's pressure points, rather than denying or running, enabled Christ to meet His "stressful reality" head on. The reality He faced was death on a cross, one of the most painful and severe ways of dying. In seeking God's will, He asked His Father to remove the cup of death. Yet Christ wanted God's will to be done rather than His, regardless of the cost. His healthy emotional responses give grounding and stability for our emotional responses. Yes, on Mount Olive and on the cross, Jesus survived the "armpit" of a most severe agony. He's the only one who can relieve your and my times of agony. Jesus knows how to relieve our pain because His pain was relieved. In agonizing over a stressful decision, Christ gave a workable, realistic model that can be applied to our lives in helping us also deal with stressful decision making.

First, Christ faced His stressful reality head on. He did not run from, try to control, neutralize, or deny the reality of why He came to earth.

Second, Christ looked for a broader perspective in His circumstance. Through prayer He asked His Heavenly Father (His reliable Source) for needed input and then accepted God's answer.

Third, Jesus stayed with and finished the conflict. Rather than resist, He listened to God's words that His time had come to die on a cross for your and my salvation. Regardless of the cost, He accepted and became obedient to God's will.[11]

Summarizing Our Thoughts on Jesus and Stress and Agony

"So what?" So what that Jesus Christ felt agony in dealing with stress? What does that do for you? Do you struggle unsuccessfully with stressful decisions? Try using Christ's model to face your stressful reality. Like Jesus, face your stressful reality head on. Stop running or denying or trying to control. Like Jesus, look first of all to God for a broader perspective. Then if needed, look to another reliable source (preferably a mature Christian). Like Jesus, let the Holy Spirit help you stay with and finish the conflict. But remember, unless you accept the challenge to discover and connect with Jesus' emotions, His model of dealing with stressful decision making cannot benefit you! In the next chapter, we will discover how Christ dealt with the stress of grieving.

Chapter Six

Jesus Felt Emotional and Physical Suffering
in
Dealing With Stress

...For Christ also suffered for you,
leaving you [His personal] example,
so that you should follow on in His footsteps.

1 Peter 2:21 AMP

"Crucify Him! Crucify Him! Let His blood be on us and on our children! We don't want Jesus, called the Christ. Release to us instead the prisoner Barabbas" (Mt. 27:20-25 par.). It was about seven in the morning. Jesus stood in the Hall of Judgment with a cord bound around His neck and hands, like a sentenced criminal. His accusers were yelling vicious, angry threats at Governor Pilate. They wanted him to crucify this impostor without any delay. The great Jewish leaders stood on the outside because they feared being polluted from the Gentile's hall. Pilate felt agitated in being summoned at such an early hour by people he considered inferior, filled with superstitions. Clearly, he did not want to do their bidding.[1] That very morning his wife warned him to not have anything to do with this Jesus because of a bad dream she had about Him. After several unsuccessful attempts to quiet the noisy crowd and reason with them, Pilate washed his hands. This let them know he would no longer have anything to do with what he considered a cover-up. He released Barabbas to the mob and had Jesus, our Savior and Lord, whipped. Then the Governor's soldiers took Jesus, stripped off His outer clothing, and put on Him a scarlet robe. They mocked Him with "Hail, King of the Jews!" After beating and spitting on Jesus, they marched Him to Golgotha as He struggled to carry the burdensome, heavy cross. Awaiting Him was the ultimate stress from emotional and physical suffering.[2]

The Stress of Walking Through Suffering

Suffering evil from another's hands, for most of us, is like the final straw dropped onto our emotional haystack.[3] It's what usually causes our emotional fortress to crumble because the stress of "suffering" is in the eye of the sufferer. Suffering to one may not be the same to another. And more times than not, without realizing it we attempt to suffer according to our parents' modeling. If their model was harmful to them, it will be harmful for us. Our unrecognized stress is the most difficult to deal with.

In many families, emotional suffering is an everyday affair because of unhealthy, codependent relationships. Amazingly few family members recognize the stress they suffer from at the hands, or mouths, of other members. We have misunderstood Paul's intention when he said, "I have become all things to all people." Most prevalent in our society are those "stressed out" from unrecognized or denied suffering. That's one reason for such a high rate of Christians suffering from codependency stress. While stress includes both the good and bad, it means something different to each of us. Stress motivates us to be more productive in a *healthy* way, and stress motivates us to be more productive in an **unhealthy** way.[4] When the unhealthy dominates our lives, we will walk through suffering combined with an emotionally damaging stress.

The Reality of Stress in Suffering

Corrie ten Boom and her family were held prisoners during Hitler's regime because they had tried to help innocent Jewish people. In prison they suffered great pain in their bodies and emotions. Corrie battled long and hard to forgive those who sinned so greatly against her. But after winning that battle she said, "God develops spiritual power in our lives through the pressures of hard places."[5] In hard places it is easy to forget we live in a "fallen world" where satan is prince of the power of the air. He's the spirit that's now working in children of disobedience. It is easy to forget during the midst of heavy trial that because Christ suffered the stress of temptation He willingly comes to our aid when we are tempted. It's also easy to forget that when we do what is right and then must suffer for it, if we will patiently endure, this is favorable with God.

It is stressful to know we were called to suffer.[6] Are you thinking, "Is it fair for God to ask us to suffer?" Isn't that where we most often get hung up, on the *unfairness* of suffering? "God, why me? Why my children? Why my parents? I don't see others suffer like I am or have." Suffering can produce either bitterness or emotional stability; it's up to us. One of the unexpected blessings of suffering, when we cooperate with God, is its refining results. Both Job and King David testified of God's refining results in their lives. We've known many who have chosen emotional stability over bitterness as God walked them through the stress of suffering.

Are you willing to suffer for Jesus' sake? I'm usually willing, until it hurts. To suffer for the sake of Jesus calls for obedient submission. Learning obedience by "[suffering] according to the will of God" is to "entrust [our] souls to a faithful Creator in doing what is right" (1 Pet. 4:19). Is that an easy choice? No, but we aren't talking about easy. We're talking about dealing with the stress of suffering for Christ's sake. This principle often goes against our "emotional grain." When we compare good with bad, suffering seems so unfair. Yet it's helpful to remember that when God designs a time of dealing with stress, "It's better to suffer for doing right rather than for doing wrong" (see 1 Pet. 3:17).

That brings us to the other side of suffering. Each of us must admit that there are times when we cause our suffering. When we are the source of our sufferings, we must confess to the wronged person and the Lord, allowing His work of grace and forgiveness. When others are the source we still feel stressed, but there's no shame to deal with. Either way, submitting to Christ empowers us to walk through the stress of suffering. That's encouraging. For although we inherit Christ's sufferings in abundance, we also feel Christ's comfort in abundance. Simply speaking, this is a peaceful "Christ confidence" that is needed to help us function in the midst of suffering.

One Example of Emotional and Physical Suffering

Some years ago, I learned something about physical and emotional suffering because of someone else's wrong. We had three young children and lived in Illinois where I was Dean of Students at the Moody Bible Institute in Chicago. Driving home one December morning, a car broadsided our little American Rambler. As I was travelling southbound through a green light, the other driver was travelling eastbound and drove through his red light. Ice and snow covered the blacktop. When our white Rambler stopped spinning, my head and upper body lay on the street with my lower body stuck inside the car. My lungs felt like they had collapsed and my breathing came in short gasps. At that point, I wasn't sure whether or not I was alive!

Someone placed a coat under my head and called an ambulance. The hospital x-rays showed seven broken ribs, many bruises and contusions on most of my body, and a large hematomia on my right thigh. I remained in shock for several days and later could not remember any conversations. After a week the doctor released me; but there would be five more weeks of healing and recovery before I could return to work. Two ambulance attendants took me home. They carried me upstairs on a stretcher to the bedroom and literally dumped me face first onto the hospital bed we had rented, and left. For several minutes I lay in a heap, face down on my seven broken ribs. I felt excruciating pain and feared they had punctured my lungs. Jane hadn't arrived yet and all I could do was gasp for breath until I could inch myself onto my back.

During the following five weeks, Jane helped me walk through healing with loving care. The stressful situation drew the five of us even closer together. Even though we were into winter big time, I started building up my physical endurance by taking long daily walks. I regretted that our car was totalled, but a friend loaned us a car until the Lord provided us with another one. I missed my responsibilities as Dean of Students, but those weeks gave me time to experience God in a new way. Scripture regarding Christ's suffering took on new meaning. Many friends, fellow workers, and students prayed, sent cards, and telephoned me. God's grace enabled me to forgive the one who turned our lives upside down in a split second.

Driving our little Rambler out of the Moody parking lot that December Saturday morning, I did not know excruciating pain and near death awaited me. But through the Holy Spirit I was very aware of God's presence as I drove into His design. In God's timing, He brought the healing needed for me to return to my "deaning" responsibilities. I returned, refreshed spiritually as well as emotionally, physically, and mentally. Yes, we are called to suffer for Christ and if we "bear up under sorrows when suffering unjustly…this finds favor" if it is "for the sake of conscience toward God" (see 1 Pet. 2:19). Regardless of the type of suffering, Jesus Christ perfects, establishes, confirms, and strengthens us for His own glory and honor as He walks us through the suffering (see 1 Pet. 5:10).

Jesus Christ and Suffering and Stress

Just as Christ was not the source of His pressures, neither was He the source of His sufferings. Jesus Christ never forgot that He came to earth to suffer for your and my sin. Jesus, the Perfect, died for us, the imperfect. The New Testament gives numerous and specific ways for which He suffered emotionally and physically. He suffered many things from elders, scribes, and chief priests. He was rejected and treated contemptuously.

Jesus allowed Himself to be sacrificed for your and my sin, but did not threaten those who killed Him. He suffered in the flesh, once, because it was necessary for the salvation of mankind.[7]

Those a few reasons Jesus is the "supreme" example for us to follow when we are walking through the stress of suffering. Even under the most terrible afflictions, Christ was patient.[8] His priestly suffering was <u>for us</u> and for our good but not because of sin, for there was **no** sin in Him. He carried our sins in His body to the cross so that we might die to our sins and live for His righteousness. Jesus is called our example only once in Scripture. Peter was telling us that Jesus had provided a "plan" for us to carry out in detail, as we would fill in a sketch. We carry out the "plan" in order to take on His righteousness.[9] Suffering death in the flesh and then being made alive in the Spirit was the only way He could bring us to God. Was that fair that He should have to die for our sin? Just as Christ was called to suffer, and not for vain glory, so are we. Like Christ did not run from suffering but walked through it, we are to carry out His example. Have you wondered how we could possibly carry out Christ's example? He left us a practical, workable, and realistic model to use when we are walking through suffering.

First, Christ did what was right and suffered for it. Jesus patiently walked through suffering, knowing He was not the source of His stress.

Second, Christ knew that His suffering was in obedience to God's will. Jesus felt no shame while walking through stressful suffering, knowing that deceit wasn't in Him.

Third, Christ knew He suffered for the sake of righteousness. Jesus spoke no evil to His persecutors and uttered no threats. He just kept submitting Himself to God.[10]

Summarizing Our Thoughts on Jesus and Stress and Suffering

"So what?" So what that Jesus Christ walked through suffering without quitting? What does that do for you? Are you suffering evil at someone else's hands? If you feel like throwing in the towel, first try Jesus' model. Like Christ did, do what is right even though you may suffer for it. Search your heart to "see" if you contributed to the stress you are feeling. If you did, as part of the source, you can ask God's forgiveness. If you are not the source, then with Jesus' help patiently walk through your suffering. Like Christ, believe your suffering is in obedience to God's will. Like with Jesus, you need not feel shame while walking through stressful suffering, knowing that you were not deceitful. Like Christ, you can believe your suffering is for the sake of righteousness. As with Jesus, speak no evil of your persecutors or utter threats to them. Just keep submitting yourself to God. But it's your responsibility to connect with Jesus' model and let Him help you deal with suffering. In the next chapter we will discover why Jesus felt grieved in dealing with stress.

Chapter Seven

Jesus Felt Grieved
in
Dealing With Stress

And after looking around at them with anger,
grieved at their hardness of heart,
He said to the man,
"Stretch out your hand."

Mark 3:5a

"Come here to Me and hold out your crippled hand. Although this is the Sabbath, if you would like for Me to, I will heal you" (Mk. 3:1-5 par.). The Pharisees closely followed Jesus in the synagogue because they wanted to find something to use against Him. Christ knew they were scrutinizing His decisions, especially to find Him in error on the Sabbath. A short time earlier, they had confronted Him about His disciples plucking and eating ears of corn on the Sabbath. Jesus claimed the Sabbath as His own, explaining that mankind wasn't made for the Sabbath but rather the Sabbath is for us. There are times when it's okay to meet a special need on the Sabbath. That's why any part of the Law functioning to the detriment of mankind is not in harmony with Divine purpose.[1] This particular day Jesus saw a man with a crippled hand, felt compassion for him, and wanted to heal his hand. But before doing so, He paused to give the Pharisees an opportunity to also show compassion for the handicapped man. Living by the Law, though, was more important to them than feeling compassion for another in need. Having given their emotions over to a hardness of heart, the Pharisees refused to respond. Seeing and feeling their silently cold stares made Jesus feel angry and very grieved with their hardened hearts.[2]

The Stress of Dealing With Inner Grieving

Inner grieving can run the gamut from superficial annoyances or worry all the way to heartrending longing for an expression of *agape* love.

That love gives value and acceptance to another simply because each of us was created in God's image and possess His worth. Failure to feel value and acceptance toward another causes the Lord Jesus, as well as the one needing love, to feel grieved. Feeling inwardly grieved with someone causes us a disturbing level of stress.[3] In refusing to let feelings of compassion rule their hearts, the Pharisees hardened their hearts toward a fellow man as well as toward God. They preferred a hard heart of self-righteously keeping the Law, over a soft heart of compassion. This selfish behavior is what caused Jesus Christ, who oozed with compassion for others, to grieve inwardly at their hardened hearts. Dealing with difficult people during times of grief is especially stressful. It's like they're emotionally blind and cannot "see" our real inner self. Added to that, they are emotionally deaf and cannot hear our grief. Topping it off, they have damaged vocal cords from choosing the wrong time to say the wrong thing.[4] In the middle of our inner grieving is when we can expect to see them coming to add stress to our heavy grief.

The Reality of Stress in Grieving

Living under daily scrutiny from those who want to destroy us or our ministry is essentially the wear and tear of living. This is aggravated by change, busyness, criticism, difficult people, conflict, others' uncontrolled emotions, concerns, and crises. When we struggle with inner conflict because of unclear direction, trying to deal with these stressors can prove too much. We find ourselves doing things we don't want to do or failing to do things we need to do.[5] That reality is as old as the Biblical Paul and gives us grief like it gave to him. Any reality that causes us to feel anxious, confused, sorrowful, or perplexed is stress and affects our emotional, spiritual, physical, and mental capacities. In short, stress is any reality that blurs our focus on Jesus Christ and causes us to lose the calming peace of God. That's why we need to become aware of what stress is and how it affects us, and avoid undesirable grief whenever possible.[6]

Inward grieving of any kind is not handled well in the Christian community at large. We have failed to observe and connect with Christ's healthy emotional responses. Therefore, our emotions are all over the place. Overall, we don't have healthy boundaries or adequate expressions for our emotional life, especially grieving. We, for the most part, no longer grieve over our sin or others'. That's why more and more immoral, unethical politicians are elected to office. We've believed the lie that "tolerance" rather than Christ's righteousness should be today's standard bearer. We must remember that Jesus was **angry** and *grieved* over the Pharisees' sin-hardened hearts. If we want His blessing, we must be willing to go through the stress of grieving over sin and turning from it. That's the only standard we dare lift up, regardless of the stress.

Examples of Stressful Inner Grieving

The stress of Marsha's[7] inner grieving feels at times like alcohol poured on an open sore. She pleads, "Where is God? Why does He continue to allow people to hurt me?" Next-door neighbors violently stole her childhood innocence. In order to survive emotionally and mentally, Marsha repressed the memories. As a result, she lived with an almost non-existent self-esteem, thinking of herself only as bad. Yet, she did not know why. Marsha coped fairly well as a teenager unless she had to deal with major change. Those circumstances seemed to aggravate her inner grieving over the loss of childhood innocence, which manifested as anger and rebellion. Since Marsha's parents didn't know of the horrible violations, they couldn't understand her behavior.

After marriage, patterns of feeling unloved and having exaggerated fears began to cover Marsha and her relationships. Finally, in her early thirties repressed memories began to surface. Each time a new memory flooded Marsha's mind, the same horrendous fears she had felt as a child devastated her. Uncontrollable crying and shaking overwhelmed her for several minutes, making it almost impossible for her to talk or describe what she was feeling and remembering. Marsha's parents tried to feel with her and comfort her. But her husband became even more distant. He withdrew from the marriage and eventually filed for divorce.

Even though Marsha knows and loves the Lord Jesus Christ, her inner grieving often feels almost too heavy to bear even with God's help. She can relate to Christ's inner grief over the Pharisees' *hardness of heart* when He wanted to heal a crippled hand. She also has felt others' lack of compassion and understanding. Critical and impatient Christians still misunderstand those people, like Marsha, who hurt very deeply yet try so hard to deal with their inner pain. Frequently, hurting Christians trying to express their pain through legitimate anger or frustration are met with condemning and quick answers or solutions. "Just read the Bible more and have more faith." This type of insensitive response, lacking in compassion, causes additional stress for hurting people.

In a different way, Becki has felt insensitive responses and a lack of compassion during a time of inner grieving. Some tried to get her healed instead of listening, praying, and weeping with her. As a child and young teen, she was full of enthusiasm and energy. At 15, when Becki started feeling pains in her left leg, she shrugged it off as growing pains. As the pain increased, doctor exams, x-rays, and extensive testing began. In her sixteenth year, she learned that her left leg could no longer remain with her. Surgery would take it from her in just two weeks. To a high school junior in the middle of track season, those words swung a stunning blow. Becki determined to make every minute of those last two weeks count. She ran and exercised as much as possible while at the same time prepared her mind and emotions. Becki came to peace with God before surgery and believes that He chose her for something special. "I had always known God had a design for my life, as He does for us all. Now He was showing me what that design looked like—it was one-legged."[8]

Through tears, grieving, and loss, Becki began to feel honored and excited that God gave her the privilege of serving Him in a very unique way. Now she understands that disabled people are very normal, and have struggles similar to those of abled people. When asked why she wasn't angry or depressed after surgery, Becki would tell them. "My relationship with Christ gives me a higher purpose than just what I could accomplish with my physical body. After all, I have given my life to God; it was really His leg that was lost, not mine."[9] While Becki still at times grieves her loss, she looks at life from God's perspective and sees it as a challenge. She's grateful for God's special emotional healing that took the stress out of healthy inner grieving.

Jesus Christ and Grieving and Stress

Christ lived with disappointments and was acquainted with inward grieving. Yet, He was not filled with bitterness. He was filled with compassion; that's why He wanted to heal the man with a crippled hand. But the accusing Pharisees' hardened hearts and refusal to *feel* compassion angered Christ. His intense grief over their hardness gave Him a heavy heart. Jesus' burden caused Him the stress of having to confront sin. Nevertheless, Christ did not let their judgmental scrutiny and hardened hearts keep Him from healing the man's crippled hand. In so doing, He modeled how to deal with stress by expressing healthy inward grieving. His model is for each of us in our own times of stress, as well as feeling with others in their pain.

First, Christ owned His emotions. He openly expressed anger and grief over the Pharisees' stubborn and hard hearts.

Second, Christ felt what He felt. He did not pretend that the Pharisees' lack of compassion was okay. He did not "tolerate" their sin; Christ felt angry with them.

Third, Christ did not allow His anger to turn to bitterness. He expressed it and then did something constructive about His inward grieving.[10] One noteworthy point to remember is that Christ's anger and grief did not make Him emotionally inoperable. He expressed appropriate emotions for the occasion and then continued with His responsibilities.

Helping Others Deal With the Stress of Inner Grieving

When we see others who need encouragement to deal with inward grieving, we can follow the above model of Jesus Christ.

First, encourage the one grieving to own his/her emotions by "telling" about the hardened heart who caused the pain. Grieving people need a friend or loved one to sit quietly and listen without showing impatience or a judgmental attitude.

Second, encourage the one grieving to feel what he/she feels. Grieving individuals need a friend or loved one to give encouragement, acceptance, and time for healing.

Third, encourage the one grieving to express a healthy anger. But, encourage the grieving one to prevent anger from being stored up and turning to bitterness by "doing something constructive" about their undeserved hurt. Constructive action will help control and reduce the anger level, helping the individual to do what is necessary in dealing with inward grieving over emotional pain and loss. But our listening, feeling, and helping must be filled with Christ's wisdom and compassion.

Summarizing Our Thoughts on Jesus and Stress and Inner Grieving

"So what?" So what that Jesus felt grieved in dealing with stress? What does this do for you? Do you struggle unsuccessfully in trying to deal with others' hard hearts? Do you need help with inward grieving? Like Christ did, own your emotions and grieve over your hurt. Like Christ did, feel what you feel. Don't pretend that the person's lack of compassion was okay, and don't "tolerate" their sin. Express a healthy anger over your emotional pain and loss. Spend a limited time grieving over the stubborn, hard hearts of those responsible for your hurt. Like Christ, do not allow your anger to turn to bitterness. You can help control your anger and inward grieving by doing something constructive, under the Holy Spirit's guidance, about others' sinful behavior. You may need to talk out the hurt;

seek prayerful support; seek financial support; seek legal advice; or try Scriptural reconciliation. Constructive action can reduce our anger level. It is your responsibility to connect with Christ's emotions so He can help you make sense out of this crazy world. In the next chapter we will discover why Jesus felt compassion for those moving through trials.

Chapter Eight

Jesus Felt Compassion
for
Those Moving Through Trials

And seeing the multitudes,
He felt compassion for them,
because they were distressed and downcast
like sheep without a shepherd.

Matthew 9:36

"Jesus, filled with compassion, touched a leper and healed him" (Mt. 8:2-3 par.). Leprosy! That dreaded, degrading disease had covered the man slowly and now weakened him as he knelt before Jesus for cleansing and healing. Jesus felt tired and somewhat weary. He had spent days and days ministering compassion non-stop to people by healing various diseases and driving out many demons as He traveled throughout Galilee. Needing rest and refreshing, Jesus and His disciples boated over to a desolate place. Hours before, Herod had commanded that John the Baptist's head be brought to him on a platter. When the disciples of Jesus learned of this, they took John's body, laid it in a tomb, and gathered around Jesus. After reporting that sadness to their Master, He suggested they boat to a quiet place and get some rest. They hoped their boat trip would be made in secret, for they actually had not even had time to eat. To their dismay, the very people from whom they needed to escape for a while saw them sailing away. Eager to hear more from Jesus, thousands ran toward the deserted destination that the disciples were boating to.[1] When Jesus walked ashore, He saw more than five thousand eager people and "felt compassion for them, because they were...like sheep without a shepherd" (Mt. 9:36).

Feeling Compassion for Others Moving Through Trials

The compassion Christ felt is the same emotion we feel when we're moved in the inward parts to feel compassion for another.[2] Most agree that compassion is "the emotion most frequently attributed to Christ...It is his expression of deep love when confronted by the desperate need of fallen men and women."[3] Since compassion is a movement in the inward parts to help meet a need, it's been described as "love in action." When we fail to let our inward parts be moved with sympathy or kindness or mercy, compassion ceases to be love in action. We see an example of this in First John 3:17 (KJV): "But whoso hath this world's good, and seeth his brother have need, and shutteth up his bowels of compassion from him, how dwelleth the love of God in him?" John is not encouraging a codependent relationship where we do for others what they can and need to do for themselves. Actually, he's encouraging us to **not** shut off those feelings but rather *feel* an active compassion for others.

The Reality of Compassion

Compassion has been described as the times when we feel sorrow for another's suffering or trouble and are moved with an urge to help. From India, Mother Teresa amazes us with her show of compassion. Carrying a bucket of water, giving a smile, or showing some other simple kindness she says makes up compassion. Besides trying to understand or share one's suffering, it's how much *agape* love we give that determines the depth of compassion. Others see compassion as "doing good" without the "inward feeling" and thus misunderstand the basic thought behind Matthew 7:12. Jesus said, "Therefore, however you want people to treat you, so treat them." He is talking, first, about a heart attitude and not necessarily *doing*. An elderly woman I know wasn't taught the truth of this verse. Instead of grasping the idea of just being kind, she thought the basic meaning meant to "buy" things for others. As a result, several whom she thought were her friends began to financially take advantage of her. Her "doing good" was from false guilt, rather than compassion.

There are five different words from numerous verses of the compassion family used in the New Testament, which show various kinds of experiences.[4] Anyone who desires to cultivate the compassion of Jesus Christ can think on this five-point, life-changing prayer:

1) Father, let me see Jesus' compassion for people. 2) Jesus, help me believe You have the same compassion for me. 3) Jesus, help me see people as You see them. 4) Jesus, help me to feel like You feel. 5) Lord Jesus, help me to express my knowledge and feelings through affirming action for others.

Praying and applying this prayer will help us use Christ's model for feeling and showing compassion.

One Example of Compassion

While Jesus Christ walked on this earth, people experienced His compassion from Him directly. Today, while moving through trials, we experience much of Christ's compassion from those He speaks to by the Holy Spirit. For even today, from His throne, Christ looks down and His compassionate nature is aroused by the sight of individuals feeling distressed while moving through trials. Moreover, when He speaks to us, our obedient response through compassion helps others become recipients of Jesus Christ's compassion—like with Eleanor.

Some years ago, Eleanor came for counseling. She had taught school for three years; one of those was in Ivory Coast, West Africa. Eleanor decided to go back for more schooling to work on her Master of Arts degree at Talbot Seminary, one school of Biola University in southern California. At age 27, she had just been diagnosed with breast cancer. During the following two-and-one-half years, she learned much about God, herself, and others. In Eleanor's love for the Lord, she determined to honor God and allow Him to walk her through the cancer experience. She said once, "I am literally staking my life on God." This Eleanor did as she received Jesus Christ's compassion through others, who were "moved in the inward parts" to befriend her.

Once, in talking about how the Lord was supplying her financial needs one step at a time she said, "I'm in graduate school now. I don't always know how I am going to pay for the next month's rent, but I know God will work it out." One of the many ways God met Eleanor's financial needs as a Talbot student was through a couple who offered her free room and board. Another, was being awarded the "Gordon Johnson Scholarship" for one year. One of her jobs was lifeguard and swim instructor at the Biola pool. After graduating from Talbot, Eleanor signed a teaching contract. The next day she learned her body was in an advanced case of cancer, which covered the liver. This had come just a little over one year from the original diagnosis.

Through that two-year period, Eleanor did not try to reduce, dilute, change, or deny a troublesome circumstance. Rather, she *faced* or *acknowledged* the reality of breast cancer as its ugly tentacles spread slowly throughout her body attaching to different organs. During that time, Jesus Christ showered Eleanor with compassion. He used her mother, sister, several aunts, the couple she lived with, and close friends to help offset some of the emotional and physical pain. She *gained a perspective* much broader than the cancer through studying Scripture, praying to the Lord, writing in her journal, and receiving encouragement from others. Eleanor *clung to hope.*

> "Please do not worry about me. I'm doing just fine. I have a 500 percent peace about dying. I'm actually looking forward to bowing on my knees and worshipping Jesus like I would look forward to Christmas as a kid. I'm not afraid one bit. I look at it as a new experience I've never had before—preparing to meet Jesus face to face!"[5]

In December of that year, experiencing the ultimate compassion, Eleanor was released from all pain and she met Jesus Christ face to face.

Jesus Christ and Compassion and Trials

Compassion, to Jesus, is not just a *feeling.* Jesus Christ felt a profound "internal movement" in His emotional nature when He saw the distress of both individuals and crowds as they moved through trials. Compassion is never impartial; it always has a target. Each time Christ felt compassion for others, He responded with some sort of intervention in their lives. Christ, at times, met their needs by Himself; at other times, He involved others to help Him. He used creative ways in reaching out. At times He saw people "like sheep without a shepherd" and ministered to their various needs. Sometimes He responded to the hungry with food, to the sick with healing, and to the bereaved with comfort. Jesus occasionally raised individuals from the dead and cast out demons from those tormented and demonized. He provided sight for some of the people who were blind. Christ's actions always corresponded with His emotions in walking people through trials. The God-man felt, looked, and acted appropriately in each occasion.

Besides His compassion, Christ had a merciful heart, felt deep affection, and expressed tender mercies in refreshing others' hearts. In the face of others' sin, Jesus showed great self-restraint. He never seemed horrified or hysterical. He did not yell and seldom showed astonishment at sin. Christ's reaction in the presence of sin is strength, not weakness, and His attitude is never mere disgust. Sin caused mankind to hate Jesus without cause. They mocked, rejected, and spat contemptuously on the God-man. When the devil could do no more, our sin crucified Him. Even then Jesus begged, "Father, forgive them; for they do not know what they are doing"

(Lk. 23:34a). He gives His unbelievable "supreme compassion" to all who need to be saved from sin.[6]

The type of compassion Jesus felt, being moved in the inner parts to meet a need, is used in the New Testament several times. Those verses describe Jesus' response to others moving through trial. In using His example, we first must make sure we have not for whatever reason cut off our inward emotions of pity or sympathy or kindness or mercy. Relating to others through coldness or anger or hostility because of what someone has done to us is not Christ's model. That behavior is the opposite of a forgiving, merciful heart. We must remember that inward emotions of sympathy or kindness or mercy can be kept alive and active. We keep them alive by using Jesus Christ's model of compassion in relating to others.

First, Jesus felt a deep, inward movement of compassion for those moving through trial. He did not deny or turn off His emotions of sympathy, kindness, and mercy. He allowed them to flow freely in relating to others.

Second, Jesus looked at each situation and determined the need and solution. He neither ignored individual needs nor compared or shrunk them. He related to each hurting person with honor and dignity.

Third, Jesus met each need in a way that was best for the individual or group or circumstance. He first of all used what was at His disposal under the Holy Spirit's creative guidance in meeting that need.[7] He neither showed partiality nor encouraged codependency.

Summarizing Our Thoughts on Jesus and Trials and Compassion

"So what?" So what that Jesus Christ felt compassion for those moving through trial? What does this do for you? If you did not receive compassionate parenting and desire to feel more compassion for others, use Jesus Christ's creative "love in action." Like Jesus, you can learn to feel a deep, inward movement of compassion for those moving through trial. That's the opposite of turning off your emotions of pity, sympathy, kindness, and mercy. Like Jesus did, look at each situation and determine the need and solution for relating to each hurting person with honor and dignity. Like Jesus, you can learn to discern between codependency and compassion. When in your means to do so, you can meet needs in a way that's best for each individual or group or circumstance. But you must accept the responsibility to discover and connect with Jesus' emotions or He cannot help you have compassion. In the following chapter we will discover why Jesus felt sympathy for those moving through trials.

Chapter Nine

Jesus Felt Sympathy
for
Those Moving Through Trials

For we do not have a high priest
who cannot sympathize with our weaknesses,
but one who has been tempted in all things as we are,
yet without sin.

Hebrews 4:15

"Do not let sin harden your hearts. Remember Jesus, in whom you hope, and His sinless model as your High Priest" (Heb. 4:7,15-16 par.). The High Priest gave unselfishly of His time and energy to others as He moved through life, for He knew that moving through trials was painful. From birth until the resurrection, Jesus moved from one heavy trial into another. He was accused of a variety of evils, from being a glutton and drunkard to being possessed by Beelzebub, prince of demons. Our High Priest had been actually accused of casting out demons by the power of Beelzebub. This wide variety of emotional and spiritual suffering as He moved through 33 years had developed within Him a deep sympathy for others walking through pain. He was indeed a High Priest who could and did understand our weaknesses.[1] He felt a *fellow feeling* with our infirmities, since He was tempted in every way like we are. Jesus, our great High Priest, can and does sympathize with our weaknesses because He knows what it feels like to suffer from the devil's persistent pressure to sin. But the good news is that He **did not sin**, even once (see Heb. 4:15).

Expressing Sympathy to Others During Times of Trial

Giving in to trials and pressures has stripped us of time, energy, or desire to use Christ's model in sympathizing with others during hard times.

Sympathy is basically the emotion that covers us when we feel the same feeling as, or for, or with, another.[2] That is Christ's way of sympathizing with us. There is significant difference between feeling compassion and feeling sympathy. Those needing sympathy want someone to sit and listen, then feel for and with them. Those needing compassion want someone to feel with them, look at their needs, and then act on their behalf. We can be better equipped if we understand the difference. Sympathy sits and listens, then feels with the one with emotional need. Compassion feels with, looks at needs, and then acts on behalf of the one in need. On the flip side, in our times of need we must be willing to *receive* so that others may give to us when we need sympathy. Some Christians are so entrenched in "doing for others" they cannot allow others to do for them. It is very interesting to note that the only time sympathy is used of Jesus Christ in Scripture we're told that He "sympathizes" with our weaknesses. In other words, He sits or spends time with us, listens to us, and then *feels* with us. Yet, His example of showing sympathy is just the opposite of that shown in much of today's Church.

The Reality of Sympathy

Sympathizing with others is a two-way choice; we "feel" with others and they "feel" with us. Yet, a deeper side of sympathy is when we suffer with another who is moving through trial.[3] Peter learned from his relationship with Christ that we are to live in harmony with one another. Often that calls for feeling sympathetic toward others. Paul recognized this when he commended the Hebrews for their sympathy to prisoners. He told us that we are not only to bear our own burdens, but we are to bear the burdens of others. (See Galatians 6:2,5.) This dual responsibility is a common sharing of sympathy with each other. Being willing to suffer with another is not an easy life. Yet, Christ designed the dual responsibility of bearing both our burdens and others' burdens to help us develop an inner emotional self-control. A well-balanced "inner life" will motivate us to give and receive sympathy, instead of cultivating a cult-of-self attitude. When we function out of self-centeredness, we will have no concern for others' need of sympathy.

Using a Christ-Designed Community to Express Sympathy

Jesus designed a helpful, healthy way for Christians to restore or reinstate a Sister or Brother with sympathy.

Brethren, if any person is overtaken in misconduct or sin of any sort, you who are spiritual—who are responsive to and controlled by the Spirit—should set him right and restore and reinstate him, without any sense of superiority and with all gentleness, keeping an attentive eye on yourself, lest you should be tempted also (Galatians 6:1 AMP).

This sympathy comes from being united with Christ. Many fail to understand what it means to be united in Christ, or to have Christ in us. By the Holy Spirit's power, Christ dwells in the justified soul born of God. Both Christ and the Holy Spirit make known to us our Father's love (see Jn. 14:7-24). From experiencing His *agape* love, we can turn from self-centeredness to express real sympathy to others.

Trying to express sympathy is usually more effective in small support-type groups versus large congregations. Small groups within the Church at large operated in New Testament days, but disappeared at some point in history. Some 30 years ago "Body Life" started a resurgence of small groups in the Church, which continue to grow in popularity and helpfulness.[4] These small groups are needed to help build times of closeness, sharing, and trust within each local church. "The Spirit carries on Christ's work calling, gathering, transforming persons into likeness to Christ, communicating to them the benefits of redemption."[5] We can show this transformation in small groups where a genuine Christ-designed sympathy is needed.

Unity with Christ through the Holy Spirit's power indwelling us believers is what motivates and energizes the whole Body of Christ. The Holy Spirit, referred to as the *Paraklete*, has the role of coming alongside us as a friend or counselor to take our part, always lending aid as a partaker in our cause.[6] He sets us free from self-centeredness so we can sympathize with others. His power enables us to come alongside hurting Sisters and Brothers just as He comes alongside to aid or support us. Usually this "coming alongside" others can happen more freely and sincerely in small support groups. I call the small group a Christ-designed Community.

This Community idea includes love, *agape*; fellowship, *koinonia*; and church or coming together, *ekklesia*. *Agape*, is the caring concern we feel for one another that gives a foundation of love to Community. *Koinonia*, is the fellowship and joint participation and sharing together that we enjoy and gives strength to Community. *Ekklesia*, is a called-out group of people in an assembly or a gathering together that we share and gives uniqueness to Community.[7] In combining these three ideas, we have a unique design for the Christian Community. In other words, the Body of Christ comes together, *ekklesia*, to share our lives, *koinonia*, because of concern for each other, *agape*.

Although some of us have experienced this unique sharing in meaningful ways through small groups within the local Church, many have not. With many people suffering in the Body of Christ, we can't afford to be ignorant of or to ignore these three Scriptural ideas any longer. We need many small support groups within the local Church, like the "Overcomers" that is designed for emotionally hurting people.[8] All of us fit into that category one way or another, sooner or later. Coming together, to share our lives, because we are concerned for each other, will encourage us to show (as well as receive) sympathy to those moving through trial.

Using Sympathy in Restoring One Another

One very special couple we've known for 30 years knows what moving through trial is like. One heavy trial is going through the shame and ridicule usually heaped on a Brother or Sister when some weakness is learned and exposed. Often, instead of coming alongside to give aid, a feeling of paranoia spreads its ugly tentacles over the local Christian community. Rather than praying for and trying to "aid" the hurting Christian in need of restoration, most of us seem to withdraw into an emotional cocoon. We take the attitude, "I can't let them see my weaknesses; they'll do the same to me." Any vulnerability or accountability that had found its way into the Body of Christ is replaced by masking and pretending on a widespread scale. The hurting Brother or Sister stands before us exposed, with no one to dress and cover emotional wounds.

Tom and Clare experienced both sides of the restoration coin. They were in what we call "full-time ministry." With a widening emotional distance between them, Clare began to suspect that Tom was spending time with another woman. She was right. For whatever reasons, there had been more than one woman filling the time and space in Tom's life that belonged only to Clare. She went to a trusted couple in their church and told them. They wanted to help, but took the wrong route. Their pastor thought the right route was to call Tom and Clare before the deacon board. However, instead of using Christ's sympathy plan described in Galatians 6:1, most of the board could not handle knowing one of their leaders had fallen. Men who were supposed to be filled with *agape* love, attacked and criticized rather than listening in order to give forgiveness and restoration.

Two lost verbal control and actually cursed Tom, completely shattering any hope for restoration and fellowship.

The pastor took control and asked one of his trusted, valued elders to come alongside Tom to spend time comforting, sharing, exhorting, and loving him. Their time together spanned a two-year period where Tom expressed his anger, humiliation, confusion, and sadness. Another man, a deacon, provided Tom with a place to stay during a three-month separation from Clare. As Tom felt acceptance, forgiveness, and *agape*, he was able to receive Scriptural exhortation. God provided a competent Christian counselor to help Clare with her emotional needs. He also spent about three years with them as a couple. He helped them walk through a much-needed time for renewed understanding of the marriage relationship. New trust, confidence, and wholesome love began to develop between Tom and Clare.

At a point in time, their elder/friend recommended Tom and Clare be welcomed back into fellowship with prayer and laying on of hands. They remember that time with gladness and appreciation. While their elder/friend had never helped walk someone through restoration, he told them the Lord assured him it could be done. He believed in Tom, appreciated his qualifications for ministry, and believed God would restore him. Tom never felt any condemnation from him, only acceptance, forgiveness, and *agape*. This is Christ's sympathy plan of restoration from Galatians. Under the Holy Spirit's guidance and with Christ-designed sympathy, Tom and Clare walked through a fiery trial to recovery and restoration.[9] They continue to walk in service to the Lord and to one another, knowing the importance of giving genuine sympathy to others.

Jesus Christ and Moving Through Trials and Sympathy

Jesus Christ, our High Priest, "understands our weaknesses, since He had the same temptations we do, though He never once gave way to them and sinned" (Heb. 4:15 TLB). His heart is not cold toward our weaknesses; rather, Christ feels a "fellow feeling" with us. Feeling with each other rather than condemning or judging will help *restore* the Christian community Christ intended. It's Christ's way of sympathizing with us in our weaknesses during time of trial. On the whole, we have miserably failed to sympathize with each other's weaknesses. Do I suggest we excuse or deny sin? No.

Our High Priest knows that like a roaring lion satan roams to and fro over the universe. He seeks individuals to drag into his lair of temptation from every culture and walk of life. Jesus knows it is hard for us to resist the devil's pressure from "the lust of the flesh and the lust of the eyes and the boastful pride of life" (1 Jn. 2:16). Christ does not excuse or wink at our sin. But because He suffered the devil's persistent pressure to sin, Christ **feels** for us when we *feel* the devil's persistent pressure to sin. Rather than dwelling on one another's sin of giving in to satanic temptation, we need to dwell on Christ's *sympathy* with us. He does not despise our weaknesses. Christ experienced temptation, but He remained **sinless**. The pressure to sin gives Him understanding of our weaknesses; this provides us with hope and strength. Christ's sympathizing with us in hard times motivates us to sympathize with others during their hard times.

Understanding and accepting this truth shows us we are called to "see" in each other a Christlike nature, to believe in each other as saints (Brothers and Sisters), and to build up each other.[10] That basically is practicing Christ's model of feeling <u>for</u> and <u>with</u> another as we move through trial, irregardless of who is to blame.

First, Jesus does not excuse sin. But He understands humanity's weaknesses in the face of satan's persistent pressure to sin.

Second, Jesus understands our weaknesses and sympathizes with us. He feels with us because of *suffering* from satan's persistent pressure to sin.

Third, Jesus, through His suffering, showed us how to resist satan's temptations. Through the Holy Spirit's power He resisted the devil's evil, persistent pressures to sin and never once gave way to them or sinned.[11] Christ's model of feeling *for* and *with* us provides a practical and workable way for us to feel sympathy, as well as to express sympathy to others.

Summarizing Our Thoughts on Jesus and Trials and Sympathy

"So what?" So what that Jesus felt sympathy for those moving through trials? What does that do for you? Do you lack motivation to show the same *sumpatheo* that Christ felt? Try using His model. Like Jesus, don't excuse your or others' sin. Remember your weakness in the face of satan's persistent pressure to sin, and consider the weakness of others. Like Jesus does not despise your weakness but sympathizes with you, feel a "fellow feeling" with others in their weaknesses as they face satan's persistent pressure to sin. Like Jesus did, resist satan's temptations through the Holy Spirit's power. Although Christ suffered from the devil's evil persistent pressures, He did not sin. It's your responsibility to connect with Christ's model so He can strengthen you spiritually and emotionally. Then you can sympathize with others moving through trial. In the next chapter, we will discover why Christ feels love in all relationships.

Chapter Ten

Jesus Felt (*Agape*) Love
in
All Relationships

Just as the Father has loved Me,
I have also loved you; abide in My love,
... This is My commandment,
that you love one another,
just as I have loved you.

John 15:9,12

It is finished (Jn. 19:30). The tense, bruised, and bleeding body of Jesus relaxed as He released His spirit into God's hands. He felt no anger. He felt no resentment. His was a pure faith, a completed love. Joseph of Arimathea, His disciple in secret from fear of the Jews, asked permission from Pilate to take and bury the body of Jesus. He and his helpers gently lifted Jesus' lifeless body from the cross. In so doing, they noticed that not a bone of Christ was broken; but they saw His spear-pierced side still oozing water and blood. With shaking hands they lovingly wrapped Jesus in a linen cloth, as their salty tears washed His body. Reverently, they carried His lifeless body to a tomb that had never been used and gently laid it there. Now that Christ the Teacher was dead, hope turned to despair for His followers. Mental numbness slowly settled over them like a thick, soupy cloud. They could not understand that this beloved dead Teacher would return to them as their beloved *alive* Savior and Lord. But in three days they would understand that He had loved them to the highest degree, through the self-sacrificing love He showed in His death.[1]

Expressing Feelings of Agape (Love) in Friendships

Self-sacrificing love is what enables humanity to function in society, rather than to explode. Although the world doesn't understand, it is this *agape* love that helps us accept one another.[2] This type of love we need to keep in prominent view as the impulse and standard, which Christ asks from His people.[3] Galatians 5:22 tells us that this self-sacrificing, accepting love is produced within us by the Holy Spirit. It is to become the "essence" for our life in Jesus Christ. To describe our feelings, we use the one word, *love*. But Greeks used the words *agape, phileo, stergos,* and *eros* to describe their feelings. Only *phileo* and *agape* are used of Jesus in the New Testament. These types of love are losing ground to a "cult of self," and are fast becoming a lost art.

The Reality of Our *Agape* (Love) Emotions

Picture, with me, a pyramid divided horizontally into four sections. Covering the whole bottom section of this emotions pyramid is *agape* love, which gives a feeling of preciousness and acceptance, providing security and stability. Spreading over the next upper section is *phileo* love, which gives a feeling of unimpassioned friendly affection or fondness for pleasurable qualities in another. Occupying the third and even smaller section is *stergos* love, which gives a feeling of natural affection—including kindness, forgiveness, and sympathy. Sitting at the top and smallest space is *eros* love, which gives a feeling of attraction of one sex for the other. If we base a relationship on an inverted emotions pyramid, the unstable and fragile feelings of *eros* will topple with the slightest wind of controversy. Yet, the strongest winds and most horrific storms cannot budge a pyramid base founded on a self-sacrificing, accepting love.

Some of us, along with parents, peers, grandparents, or other relatives, lived and worked and served during World War II. While not all were Christians, many people for the most part operated under the umbrella of a benevolent, self-sacrificing love. Most workers did not enjoy a vacation time, health benefits, or retirement in comparison with today. Roof overhead, food on the table, couple sets of clothing, and two strong legs for walking were the extent of many people's petitions. Compared with today's average grumpy workers, contentment was widespread. Many times satisfaction came from helping a neighbor. Such choices fulfill Christ's commandments to love our neighbor, be kind to others, and love the Lord God.

Can we complain because Jesus asks from us a self-sacrificing love? Didn't He choose and appoint us to go and bear fruit for Him? But "bearing fruit" is more than just doing the work of an evangelist. That limited view overlooks the love of benevolence. Many misunderstand why Paul says, "If I...do not have love, it [good works] profits me nothing" (1 Cor. 13:3). As a result, they do all kinds of "works" trying to receive a *feeling* of being accepted and loved. He isn't saying <u>work</u> for love; rather he's saying that in order to love others for themselves, we must first have felt an accepting love from another. That is why healthy parental love is so important for a child. Sometimes those who have **not felt** loved will argue and say it doesn't matter. They fail to realize that when children do not "feel" love's true essence, an emotional vacuum is formed within them. In trying to fill it, they "work" for love. And, arguing about love rather than letting God's love flow into that vacuum emotionally cripples us and keeps us from loving.

The "love of benevolence" Paul speaks of is not so much a love of finding good as that which intends good. Self-sacrificing love is the foundation of its twin companion, compassion.[4] Paul is telling us that if we've <u>never known</u> accepting/approving love, we **cannot give** accepting/approving love because we *don't know how.* We can't give what we don't have. Yet, Christ's compassion for our good pours out *agape* "in our hearts through the Holy Spirit" (see Rom. 5:5; Gal. 5:22). That's one way God "reparents" us and fills our empty hearts crying out for acceptance and love we've never known.

Another way He reparents us is through the loving acceptance and encouragement from Christian Brothers and Sisters. Yet, love is two-sided; it's not only receiving, love is giving. In modeling *agape*, Christ gave us responsibility. He told us to love others as **He** loved us (see Jn. 15:9,12). One motivation to love comes from His calling us "friends," which shows that we're the recipients of His love. Thus, when we receive accepting love from Brothers and Sisters in Christ, we then have love to give. We love because we are loved. Having and feeling love empowers us to give to others, even to sacrifice. Self-sacrificing, benevolent love given according to Christ's design profits us and those to whom we give because we are being connected with His healthy emotions.

Beginning when my sons and daughters were small, I would hug them and say, "I want you to know I love you just as you are." Since my parental love to them was respectful and appropriate, even in their teens they didn't mind my hugging them in front of their friends. Today we still give each other warm, affectionate hugs. In spite of their childhood tragedies, I believe those healthy hugs helped my sons and daughters to begin connecting with Christ's healthy emotional responses. All four of them have been empowered to develop relationships with both males and females.

One Example of Expressing *Agape* (Love) in Relationships

While many women involved with the National Organization for Women (NOW), or other feminist movements, strongly react to a sacrificial love, it is Scriptural. The Proverbs Woman in Proverbs 31:10-31 gives us one practical model. Furthermore, there are still mothers like Marsha who work faithfully to care for their children. As a single mom, she parents an 8-year-old son and a 12-year-old daughter. In teaching them responsibility with home chores and school homework, she is careful to encourage them for their efforts. She teaches them God's truths from the Bible as well as by her actions. Marsha gives her children sincere praise for who they are and the positive qualities she sees in them.

She tries to teach them kindness, mercy, forgiveness, and love by her responses to them. When they feel sad, she encourages them to talk about their disappointments. When Marsha is unkind, she asks for forgiveness and forgives them when they in turn ask for forgiveness. She plays with them, doing the fun things they like. She faithfully takes them to church and encourages them to participate in the activities provided for their age group. Marsha tries to minimize competition between her children by giving loving appreciation for their individual achievements and awards. As a single Mom, Marsha feels heavy responsibility on her shoulders. She says, "God gives me new strength daily. I believe character is being built in both me and my children through the self-sacrificial, accepting love we share."

Jesus Christ and Relationships and *Agape* (Love)

Even though Christ's actions were love motivated, only in Mark 10:21 was love attributed to Him. A rich, young ruler asked Christ the way to "inherit eternal life." After listing the Commandments, the young man said, "Teacher, all these I have observed from my youth." Jesus felt an accepting, benevolent love for him; however, Christ was unable to intervene in the man's life until he could let go of an unhealthy attachment to money. These behavior models of Christ differentiate between the actions of love and compassion. When feeling compassion for others, Christ was always moved to and able to take action on their behalf. On the other hand, when feeling *agape* for others, He tried to motivate them to unselfish action either for Him or for others.

Eros is another of the four Greek words for love not used by Jesus, and not found in Scripture. It's best defined as passion seeking satisfaction. *Eros* is not essentially an evil word. Some early Christian writers used it when referring to Divine love and to a child's love for his mother. On the flip side, some used it in pagan writings to identify the sexual love between spouses. Some say *eros* is "an overmastering passion seizing upon and absorbing into itself the whole mind."[5] C.S. Lewis wrote that *eros* is taken as the image when Christ is represented as Bridegroom to His Bride, the Church.[6] But Scripture does not back up his statement; *agape* is clearly the "Calvary" **love** Christ demonstrates in calling His Bride, the Church.

Christ's love for His Bride was called from His heart because He esteems each soul as precious. His love prizes and values His loved ones; He accepts and recognizes the worth of them. In other words, His love "elevates, ennobles, and purifies" the other loves. *Eros*, passion seeking satisfaction, is self-centered and takes rather than gives. In contrast, accepting benevolence esteems and prizes another unconditionally and gives without asking anything in return. This is Christ's love for His Bride the Church, and that's why *agape* is known as the self-sacrificing love.[7] Christ feels this type of love for us, His Bride, whether we're male or female and regardless of race or color. As His Bride, we must respond to His love in order for closeness and trust to develop between Him and us.

Jesus said clearly that those who love Him will keep His commandment to "love one another, just as I have loved you" (see Jn. 15:12). Yet, loving another unconditionally and giving without asking in return cannot be accomplished on our own. A young man who had been married for ten years told me recently how the truth of Christ's words "love one another as I have loved you" filtered his thoughts. Some months after marriage, in prayer one day he cried out, "Jesus, help me. In myself I can't love my wife as You love me." The Holy Spirit, our indwelling Helper, teaches and empowers us to love as Christ did. He assured Alan that Jesus knew his earthly strength was not sufficient. As Alan submitted to Christ, the Holy Spirit empowered him to feel a self-sacrificing benevolence for his wife. This love is devoid of sensuousness, recognizes an individual's worth, and gives acceptance. It is truly a love called out of one's heart by the preciousness of the person loved.[8] As Alan loves by those standards, he is loving as Christ loves. And whether our relationships are close, neutral, or in between, Christ modeled how to give an accepting love.

One, Christ accepts us where we are and sees us as persons of worth. That's the way we're to accept ourselves and others—regardless of race, color, church status, or employment.

Two, Christ prizes, values, and sees us as precious and that's the way we're to relate to others. But He did not call us to codependency; He does not do for us what we can and need to do for ourselves. Christ calls us to an interdependence with Him through submission, commitment, and perseverance.

Third, Christ loves in us our God-given valuable qualities and we're to look for, develop, and use them. He calls us to keep His commandments, use our spiritual gifts, and produce spiritual fruit showing our love for Him.[9] These models, when followed, will empower us to love as Christ loves.

Summarizing Our Thoughts on Jesus and Relationships and Feeling *Agape* (Love)

"So what?" So what that Jesus felt (*agape*) love in all relationships? What does that do for you? Do you need to feel more acceptance in your relationships? Do you want to see others as precious? Use Christ's model. Just as Jesus accepts you where you're at and sees you as a person of worth, relate in the same way to others. Like Jesus prizes you and values you and sees you as precious, relate in the same way to others. Like Jesus loves the God-given valuable qualities in you, so relate to others. However, the responsibility is yours to experience and connect with Jesus Christ's emotional responses. If you don't, His models cannot help you build healthy relationships. In the next chapter we will discover why Jesus feels *phileo* (love) in a few relationships.

Chapter Eleven

Jesus Felt (*Phileo*) Love
in
a Few Relationships

"Lord, behold, he whom You love [phileo] is sick."
... "Behold how He loved [phileo] him!"
... [Mary] ran...to the other disciple
whom Jesus loved [phileo].

John 11:3,36; 20:2a

"Friends, come and show Me the cave where you placed My friend Lazarus for burial" (Jn. 11:34 par.). Christ had developed friendships on different levels. The Lazarus family was only one example of His healthy friendships. Because of sharing an inner community with many things in common, Jesus had enjoyed a friendly affection with them. That's why the sisters and their friends had felt rejection when Christ didn't immediately come to comfort them. Now, Jesus was asking to see Lazarus' place of burial. Doesn't He know that after four days the normal deterioration process is oozing with a strong odor? But this would not keep Jesus from His mission of showing forth God's almighty power. Returning physical life to Lazarus gave Christ's followers a clear picture of His own forthcoming resurrection. Yet, Jesus felt a double bind. Motivated by compassion, Christ was eager to return Lazarus to life so He could teach His friends about God's power. Yet, Jesus had felt the same emotional shock of seeing a loved one die as did relatives and friends. He felt concern that when Lazarus walked from the tomb they would suffer another type of emotional shock in seeing him returned to physical life. He wanted to spare as much trauma as possible for those He liked.[1]

Expressing Feelings of Phileo (Love) in a Few Friendships

Friendship was important to the Greeks. From the heart they displayed friendship through affection, a fondness or liking, for those who displayed pleasurable qualities like those of themselves. Such is an unimpassioned and friendly love.[2] This type of love is used only three times of Jesus, and it means to feel a mutual attraction for another. Those who are involved with homosexuality and pushing for same-sex marriage are working long hours to change this unimpassioned and friendly affection into a lustful passion.[3] This "unnatural" behavior, designed by satan, has caused many to grow increasingly fearful of a healthy and normal closeness with others of the same sex. This "fear" is the dread that a healthy, normal friendship might turn into an "unnatural" and unhealthy type of friendship that God hates.

The Similarity of *Stergos* to *Phileo* and Its Need in Society

The normal, natural affection felt for another is *stergos* love. In feelings, it is very similar to the unimpassioned love of friendship and it is one of the four Greek words not used of Jesus. If we use *stergos* as a noun with the Alpha prefixed, its regular meaning of "natural affection" is made to "mean the opposite to what it meant in itself."[4] In other words, the irregular meaning becomes "without natural affection." In Romans 1, Paul very clearly describes those who had knowingly **left** their "natural affection" to behave in a sexual manner contrary to God-designed nature. Many cult-of-self individuals live **without** "natural affection." God placed within humanity "a natural movement of the soul" when He created Adam. This natural affection bonds husband with wife, parents with children, neighbor with neighbor, or people within communities.[5] Shakespeare called natural affection the "milk of human kindness." Without this type of love God has given us for others, we would destroy each other like those who are guilty of the heinous and unthinkable April, 1995, bombing in Oklahoma City. Our God-designed emotions must not be perverted either in natural affection or in unimpassioned love for others.

One Example of Expressing *Phileo* (Love) in Relationships

Females of all ages are usually recognized as having more friendships than most males. This often causes relational problems in marriage. For many long years, large portions of society have placed much of marital responsibility on women. Typically, more women than men attended church and took their children. More women than men spent special time with the children trying to teach and train them for life. More women than men stayed in the marriage rather than jumping ship. Looking down this road, we now see a turn. Many men are taking a more active part in raising their children. Since inflated living costs forced many married women into the job market, more men are sharing some of the in-house work. More men are attending church, are getting involved with church, and are trying to build healthy, *phileo* types of friendships.

Some credit for the "turn" is given to an organization called Promise Keepers. Each year in different cities and stadiums across our land, they provide times of fellowship, fun, worship, and personal challenge to men of all ages. Stadiums are filled each time with 50,000 to 60,000 men. In 1995, over 720,000 men gathered in 13 different stadiums. Promise Keepers say they want the meetings to be more than an event. They "believe God wants Promise Keepers to be a spark in His hand to ignite a worldwide movement calling men to reconciliation, discipleship, and godliness."[6] Many are reporting emotional bonding between older fathers and adult sons. New bondings between races, new acceptance for differences in opinion, and new appreciation between denominations are also reported. And it's all in the name of Jesus Christ.

Promise Keepers' new magazine just for men is designed to further help males of all ages become men of God. This work is a spiritual challenge from brotherly love that is teaching men to <u>keep</u> their promises of commitment. The "promises" include commitment to Jesus Christ, Scripture, marriage, vital relationships, purity, a local church, influencing the world, and reaching beyond racial or denominational barriers. Men keeping those promises are connecting with Jesus' unimpassioned, friendly love with mutual attraction. Like Jesus, they are feeling drawn to those who display pleasurable qualities of themselves, regardless of skin color or work status. Many men are discovering the healthy affection or fondness of others through responsibility, giving, receiving, closeness, openness, and friendship.[7] That's why the emotional healing and bonding taking place as a result of the Promise Keepers movement is having such a practical, needed impact on men. More are learning to develop **healthy**, *phileo* relationships.

Jesus Christ and *Phileo* (Love) and Relationships

Jesus shows us clearly that it's okay to feel different levels of like and love with different individuals in relationships. Although Jesus felt self-sacrificing, accepting love for all, He only felt an unimpassioned, friendly love for a few. He felt drawn to those who displayed pleasurable qualities like those of Himself. This love is "not unethical, being perfectly proper in its place...and imposes no obligations upon the one who shows this affection."[8] His purity and sensitivity in building relationships provide the best model for us to follow.

Jesus Christ felt different emotions at times for His disciples and followers, asking for nothing in return. Even among His disciples, He developed different levels of relationships. For example, Jesus feels an approving, accepting love for His disciples, friends, and all of us, His followers. And yet, for Peter, John the beloved, and Lazarus, He also felt a mutual attraction or an unimpassioned love in friendship. He showed us that different levels of relationships are normal and okay. Something noteworthy about Jesus' relationships is that His emphasis was upon the love **of** friendship, not necessarily on the person. Because a few try to pervert Christ's pure friendship model, it's helpful to remember that the emphasis of Jesus and Lazarus' friendship was upon a love of friendship which existed between them. "It is the human heart of Jesus which we see here."[9] The God-man showed us that initiating friendship rests on each of us. Yet, it's okay when we don't have time or energy for many close friends. For our help and encouragement, Jesus modeled healthy friendship in three ways.

First, while it's evident that John, Mary, Lazarus, and Martha were important to Christ, He did not place friendship above His relationship with God the Father.

Second, while it's evident that Christ enjoyed being with friends, He did not place friendship before ministry.

Third, although Christ built strong relationships through *agape* with many, He built a close bonding through *phileo* with only a few.[10]

If we want to live without excessive loneliness and experience a few enjoyable and healthy relationships, we must choose to follow His model.

Summarizing Our Thoughts on Jesus and Relationships and *Phileo* (Love)

"So what?" So what that Jesus felt *phileo* (love) for only a few people? What does this mean to you? Do you need to build a few strong friendships? Use Christ's model of not placing friendship above relationship with God the Father. Like Christ, do not place enjoyment of friendship before ministry. Like Christ, build many *agape* acquaintances and without false guilt build a close bonding through *phileo* with only a few.

But be sure to discover and connect with Christ's emotions or He cannot help you in relationships. In the next chapter we will discover why Jesus felt joy in some relationships.

Chapter Twelve

Jesus Felt Joy
in
Some Relationships

These things I have spoken to you,
that My joy may be in you,
and that your joy may be made full.

John 15:11

"Men, part of the *abundant life* I've talked about is your walking with Me in My love, producing spiritual fruit, keeping My commandments, and feeling My joy" (Jn. 15:10-11 par.). Jesus had spent many hours daily for almost three years teaching His disciples how to walk with Him and His Father. A branch cut off from the vine loses nourishment and cannot bear fruit. In like manner, to receive spiritual nourishment the disciples must stay connected to Him and keep His Word connected to them in order to produce spiritual fruit. Christ was ending His instruction time with a few thoughts about how to keep His commandments. He explained that walking in His love **is** keeping His commandments. Furthermore, Jesus told His disciples if they wanted to feel a "full joy" they must walk in His love and keep His commandments. Therefore as His "hour" was creeping close, He did not speak of His deep sorrow since His one desire was for them to have and know His love and **joy**.[1] Jesus wanted His disciples to understand how to fulfill their joy here on earth. He wanted them to know that they would feel a delight or cheerfulness by connecting with His emotions and making Him their life.[2]

Experiencing Joy in Relationships

This connection with Jesus' emotions comes through the Holy Spirit who indwells and empowers us so we can take on the mind of Christ and grow into His image. This calls for walking and living by the Spirit rather than by our fleshly desires. As this process in changing lives happens, we will learn to feel Jesus' joy. While similar, joy is not the same emotion as being glad or happy. Glad feelings depend on circumstances, either for us or others, that fit together for some kind of good. Happy feelings depend on "right happenings" that provide us with pleasure, more for us than for others. Although anyone can feel glad and happy, only Christians can feel the joy that comes from Christ. His joy provides a motivating inner force we can feel even in emotional, mental, or physical suffering to help us endure beyond our natural strength. This emotion does not depend on perfect people, happy circumstances, or something we understand. This emotion comes from connecting with Christ's joy (see Jn. 15:11; 16:22; 17:13).

The Reality of Sometimes Feeling Joy

Gladness and joy are somewhat different emotions. Both come from the heart and cannot be masked or pretended. The Greeks chose nine various words to describe joy, but we use only the one word.[3] Joy is a fruit from the Holy Spirit and can be looked at from two different perspectives. From one view it's a fleeting emotion usually produced by some expectation of or delight in good, initiated either by us or by others. From another view, joy can be felt as an ongoing cheerful and happy frame of our spirit coming from a sense of blessedness or security.[4] Joy has to do more with our affections than our reason and is seen as enthusiasm. This motivating inner force moves us out of ourselves to make us able to do and suffer much that is otherwise beyond our natural strength. We may feel joy as a fleeting emotion; however, we can also learn that over sadness, **joy** can become the normal state for Christians.[5]

Our friend, Gloria, has experienced joy over sadness. After she had birthed and raised their three children, her husband announced one day that he wanted a divorce. In addition, he declared bankruptcy keeping Gloria from receiving her rightful portion of their property. As a result, in her early fifties Gloria was left without money or a place in which to live. While seeking a job, a friend opened her place to Gloria without pay until work came. In the meantime, she was trying to wander through the maze of a divorce she had neither designed nor wanted. Although her husband abandoned her, she learned quickly that God would not do so. "I began talking out loud to Jesus and the Heavenly Father back when my separation was new.

I would say, 'God, I cannot bear this pain; the depression will consume and destroy me. Take it from me; I give it up to You. Give me back the joy of being Your child.' He does, oh He does! Joy divine is mine!'"

Depression still tries to creep back in at times, but in these moments Gloria has learned to read a Psalm or a verse from Isaiah or a portion about Jesus. He uses His Word to once again restore her joy. Joy's most meaningful moments are not felt from certain circumstances nor from being planned; rather than resulting from achievement or success, the emotion just happens. Biblical joy is *couched* between Christ's command to follow Him and obey His commandments, especially to love others (see Jn. 15:11). From that perspective, joy in relationships is unplanned but surely may be anticipated.

Another Example of How to Feel Joy

Even though Ann and Roy have felt joy with their three young daughters, Ann says she does not believe we feel joy very often. "Many confuse joy with feelings of happiness or being glad. Those feelings usually come from things or circumstances, but joy comes from within. We feel *joy* with others because of their good experiences."

Miscarriage ended Ann and Roy's first pregnancy at 16 weeks, causing much grief for them. Added to that, with each pregnancy Ann's body tried to reject the little "baby beginnings." This meant she had to spend time in a hospital to receive intravenous feedings of vitamin B_{12} and other nutrients. Ann also suffered from ongoing motion sickness, losing everything she would try to eat. Through each difficult pregnancy Ann and Roy worked together to accomplish the hoped-for reality of receiving into their arms a safe, healthy baby. As time has passed, Ann no longer remembers the pain, grief, and suffering. She agrees with the apostle John that, "A woman giving birth to a child feels the sorrow of pain because her hour has come; but when the child is born she remembers no more the anguish because of the joy that a child is born" (Jn. 16:21 par.).

Roy and Ann view each daughter as a unique personality, and feel delight "with them in their accomplishments" rather than "in what they do." One daughter has won awards in running. Once, when a jealous boy tripped her, she got up quickly and with bleeding knees ran on to win the race. Another daughter won first place recently in a Tae Kwon Do fencing competition, which she uses for safety rather than for meditation. A jealous mother with angry words tried to rob their daughter of her rightful victory. But Ann and Roy helped their daughter to "feel" her feelings of joy.

Watching their youngest entertain the family at home with her funny antics also brings cheerful feelings.

Jesus Christ and Relationships and Feeling Joy

While Christ was praying to the Heavenly Father about the disciples, He petitioned God, "May My joy be made full in themselves" (see Jn. 17:13). In talking about Jesus and joy, some have pictured Him as a lord of revelry, being frivolous, bringing festivities, being adored, and having a naive dizziness of joy. Going further, He is pictured magically as making life's hard conditions vanish at a touch.[6] In so picturing Christ, one forgets why He came to earth. Yet, Christ never lost sight of the cross where His body would be broken and His blood shed for your and my sin. This was Jesus Christ's ultimate joy. While some call Him the "Man of Sorrows," He is known more profoundly as the Man of Joy.[7] Both Gloria and Ann agree that Jesus' type of joy comes when pain or sorrow or disappointment has been turned into some type of gain.

For example, Christ was "the seed" to die, go into the ground, and rise again as our "price of victory, the ransom for many."[8] With this **joy** before Christ, "He endured the cross, despising the shame, and sat down at the Father's right hand" (Heb. 12:2 par.). Until we join Christ the Son and God the Father in Heaven, we cannot know the ultimate *joy* Jesus talked about.

> "Joy he had: but it was not the shallow joy of mere pagan delight in living, nor the delusive joy of a hope destined to failure; but the deep exultation of a conqueror setting captives free. This joy underlay all his sufferings."[9]

Feeling outward happiness and experiencing inward joy are not the same. It's been said that feeling "joy" beats being happy since happiness depends on right happenings; but even when things go wrong we can feel Christ's deep and abiding **joy**.[10] Feeling Christ's joy, however, is not an automatic response for Christians. His plan for our experiencing joy is an example for us to follow. Yet, that's not *working* for joy; it's following Christ's choices.

First, Jesus submitted to the Holy Father's authority. He did not resist or complain or argue but allowed God's pruning in His life.

Second, Jesus kept the Father's commandments. He produced great spiritual fruit for our profit and to glorify the Father.

Third, Jesus chose to abide or walk in God the Father's love. He received the Father's love which enabled Him to love us.[11]

Christ's joy is a natural outflow of the indwelling Holy Spirit who connects us to Jesus Christ and His emotions.

Summarizing Our Thoughts on Jesus and Relationships and Feeling Joy

"So what?" So what that Jesus felt joy in some relationships? What does this mean for you? Would you like to experience more joy in your life? Feeling Christ's joy is not automatic for us. As Jesus did, we must submit to the Holy Father's authority. We must not resist or complain or argue but allow God's pruning in our life. As Jesus did, we must keep the Father's commandments and produce great spiritual fruit for the profit of others and to glorify the Father. As Jesus did, we must choose to abide or walk in God the Father's love. We need the Father's love, which enables us to love others. We also must stay connected to Christ through the Holy Spirit's power. Being connected involves learning and applying Scripture, taking on Christ's thinking and emotions, and growing into His image. When you choose to discover and connect with Jesus' emotions, even in the midst of things going wrong you can feel Christ's deep, abiding joy. In the next chapter, we will discover why Jesus felt glad in a close relationship.

Chapter Thirteen

Jesus Felt Glad
in
One Close Relationship

...Lazarus is dead,
and I am glad for your sakes that I was not there,
so that you may believe;
but let us go to him.

John 11:14-15

"Tell them this sickness is not unto death. It's to honor and promote God's glory and thereby to glorify His Son" (Jn. 11:4 par.). Back to Bethany's town square for more cold water from the community well, then walking as briskly as possible without splashing from their water buckets. The cold water would help cool Lazarus' feverish face and thirsty throat. Sponging Lazarus often and cooking nutritious soup for his strength may have designed most of Mary and Martha's days. When Lazarus was too weak to stand, the sisters sent a messenger running to Jesus who was holding evangelistic meetings nearby. After reading the message, Christ apparently dismissed him with, "Don't worry." Yet, by the time the messenger returned to them with His response, Lazarus had died. Both sisters felt irritated and confused because Jesus had not immediately come to help. Wasn't He their friend? Shouldn't He have been there to comfort them? Those were the wrong questions. The Master over death knew He did not face "an impassable barrier, but a call to battle."[1] That's why in the midst of moaning and loud wailing Jesus could say that although Lazarus had died, He's "glad" He wasn't there.[2]

Feeling Glad in One Special Relationship

Through a deliberately delayed action, Christ decided He and the disciples would not rush to see Lazarus. They would stay in Bethabara two more days before travelling. During that time, Christ didn't speak of Lazarus as being dead but rather as being "asleep" and needing to be awakened. The disciples evidently thought He was confused and assured Him that sleeping would be okay for Lazarus. For, at that time, the disciples could not understand Christ's teaching about His coming resurrection. While they packed things for the journey, Christ saw their wrinkled brows and spoke to them bluntly. Jesus explained that Lazarus had died and that for their sake He was glad they were not there.[3] He said this would help them believe. That further confused the disciples. They who had witnessed His love for Martha, Mary, and Lazarus now puzzled, "How can Jesus be *glad* that He was not there to grieve with the sisters and comfort them?" They didn't know what to believe.

The Reality of Sometimes Feeling Glad

We can neither manufacture a glad feeling nor force others to be happy or rejoice. Accordingly, to stay in a state of feeling glad is neither emotionally possible nor sound Scripturally. Because all of us, according to our emotional need, respond to relationships in different ways we cannot rush others or ourselves into a time frame for feeling glad. It is sometimes difficult to feel happy, especially when dealing with controversy. During this time it's normal to wander through many valleys since emotional change or healing takes time and cannot be hurried. Jane and I have experienced this dilemma.

One of the most difficult things about controversy is feeling the stress that goes along with being misunderstood. Almost seven years ago when our adult children's repressed memories started coming up, we lived under the heavy stress of being misunderstood. Except for one couple, all those we had worshiped with for 16 years did not want to hear. Even most of my colleagues could not handle the controversial, emotional reality my family now suffered. At that point, we weren't sure that we would ever again feel glad about anything. With the passing of time, God has given much emotional and spiritual healing with understanding. In addition, we have been able to help many others who have also suffered from satanic ritual abuse. Any good that God may bring from our children's loss, however, **cannot** okay the heinous, unspeakable, unbelievable crimes forced on them. But during any type of stressful controversy we can cling to the hope that "this too shall pass." We can go on working toward emotional wholeness until we hear, "Well done, thou good and faithful servants" (see Mt. 25:23). Just the thought of that "voice" helps us have a happy feeling of *gladness*.

Examples of Sometimes Feeling Glad

Feeling a "glad" response in relationships like Christ did must be done without hurrying. Unless a controversy calls for immediate action, taking time to think through the situation like Christ did, can prove most helpful. A friend of ours died after long, painful months of suffering from horrendous cancer pain. Sometime later, his wife wrote that she could not understand everything during his illness but had slowly begun to find some answers for immediate questions. At times she doubted God's over-all plan, but she kept sorting through the puzzle pieces. She held on to the promise that God's Word would lead her and make the jigsaw puzzle of life fit together. God wasn't in a hurry with our friends; but one day He said, "Welcome home." Jeri loved her husband and was not glad he had died. But regardless of how much Jeri missed him, she was grateful God released him from the long months of cancer pain. For this she felt a deep gladness.[4]

Some years ago, Jane's father died because of a paralyzing stroke that took away his ability to talk or use his left side. While Jane grieved her father's death, she thought about God's mercy and grace that called Father Allen home after only one week of physical suffering. For that, she truly felt *glad*. Over two months later, the telephone rang at dinnertime. Mother Allen had died within minutes after having congestive heart failure. Jane's emotions now carried a double load as she walked on through the grieving process. With the passing of time, she has stated many times, "Since Mom suffered so much emotional pain during her lifetime, I'm very *glad* that God chose to take her home without any physical suffering." Jane knows she will see her parents again because they were believers and because Jesus is "the resurrection and the life" (Jn. 11:25). While Jane was not glad they had died, that hope gives her a feeling of gladness.

Jesus Christ and Feeling Glad and Relationships

Jesus Christ's life clearly shows that He did not always live in a state of gladness. A large percentage of His emotional expressions were actually just the opposite of glad. The God-man's emotions ranged from agony to peace to weeping. Yet, it's evident He did not feel anxious or pushed in regard to His emotional reality. Although the emotional pain Mary and Martha felt from Lazarus' death was equally painful for Jesus,

He did not try to rush through the experience. "Christ is never in haste: least of all, on His errands of love. And He is never in haste, because [regardless of the situation] He is always sure."[5]

When Jesus deliberately delayed in going to see His sick friend, Lazarus, He was misunderstood. Jesus was trying to prepare the disciples for His death; but without a point of reference, they could not understand. When He talked of feeling glad about Lazarus' death, Jesus' statement caused a stressful controversy and left the disciples perplexed. Yet, as they would see, "Christ feeling glad" wasn't *because* His friend had died. Christ's reason for returning physical life to Lazarus was for them to "see" and experience God's power and glory. Witnessing His power in returning life to Lazarus helped the disciples to perceive how God would one day return physical life to Christ.

This new understanding of Jesus' decisive movements in His two-day deliberate delay cleared the air and helped to reduce their stress level. In a sense, they were reminded of what King David had previously written. "Cease *striving* and know that I am God" (Ps. 46:10a). They came to understand that Lazarus' death had given Christ an opportunity to "perform a great and incontrovertible miracle."[6] This was His reason for feeling *glad*. Out of that controversy came a sound and practical model for dealing with stressful relationships.

First, Christ reasoned with others. He did not hurry or try to hurry others in the midst of misunderstanding and controversy. He took time for a sound solution through careful thought and prayer.

Second, Christ did not hide the facts. He didn't hesitate to state His true feelings in the midst of controversy and misunderstanding. In the midst of life, Christ was not always happy or rejoicing; neither did He live in a state of feeling glad. Although the disciples misunderstood His emotions and motives, He communicated clearly and calmly with them.

Third, Christ spoke the truth. He did not let the fact of others' misunderstanding His emotions or motives to deter Him. He did not give in to embarrassment or shame or others' pressure during controversy.[7] Following Christ's example for dealing with controversy can help us better relate to others and may even produce a glad feeling.

Summarizing Our Thoughts on Jesus and Relationships and Feeling Glad

"So what?" So what that Jesus felt glad in a close relationship even though He was misunderstood in controversy? Do you experience misunderstanding and controversy? Use Jesus' model. Like Christ, you need not hurry or try to hurry others in the midst of misunderstanding and controversy. You can take time for prayer and careful thought for a sound solution. Like Christ, you need not hesitate to state your true feelings. Since He was not always in a state of feeling glad, neither will you be in moving through life. Like Christ, when misunderstood you can still communicate clearly and calmly and not give in to embarrassment or others' pressure, nor allow yourself to be deterred. In the next chapter we will discover how Jesus rejoiced in one special relationship.

Chapter Fourteen

Jesus Rejoiced
in
One Special Relationship

[Christ] rejoiced greatly in the Holy Spirit,
and said,
"I praise Thee, O Father...."
Luke 10:21

"You horde of evil spirits called Legion, come out of this man. You cannot indwell another human, but I give you permission to enter that large herd of hogs" (Mk. 5:9-13 par.). Christ's unrelenting commands to unclean spirits always demanded their instantaneous obedience. He often chided them and "the power" behind them for evil inflicted on their victims. The immediate flight of the horde of evil spirits from the man to the herd caused such confusion that the hogs ran wildly down a steep hill and over a cliff. This herd, numbering almost two thousand, dropped like cannonballs into the sea. Stunned from the fall, they choked and drowned. The townspeople reacted with fear. Rather than expressing gratefulness to Christ for His intervention to free their neighbor from evil spirits, they asked Him to leave. In contrast, that man whom Christ freed from the violent horde of evil spirits wanted to go with Him.[1] Jesus instructed him however, "Go home to your people and report to them what great things the Lord has done for you, and *how* He had mercy on you" (Mk. 5:19). Today, Christ still frees us from demonic power.

Learning to Rejoice and Praise the Father

Christ taught His followers well in spiritual warfare, just as He is trying to teach us today. Setting demonized people free was commonplace with Christ and those He trained. Yet, He told them clearly, "Do not rejoice...that the spirits are subject to you, but rejoice that your names are recorded in heaven" (Lk. 10:20). In similar words, when you exercise power in Jesus' name over evil spirits don't let that be your glory or boast and don't compete with them. The power against evil spirits comes from **Jesus Christ's name**, not us. When in the "name of Jesus" evil spirits are commanded to go, they must leave an individual just as Jesus demonstrated many times in Scripture. Glory and honor for this movement belong not to us—although we have been given authority over the enemy's power—but to Jesus Christ, the God-man (see Lk. 10:19-20).

The Reality of Christians Rejoicing and Praising

Going further, Jesus Christ showed His followers that deliverance from demonic strongholds is only **one** of many movements toward spiritual wholeness. Spiritual maturity includes learning about who we are in Christ Jesus, the person and work of the Holy Spirit, how to put on the whole armor of God, how to pray in the Spirit, producing spiritual fruit, and how to rejoice in Him.[2] Biblical rejoicing includes entering into celebration and praise to the Holy Father.[3] Rejoicing is connected directly with our thoughts. We can't keep our mind on complaining, self-centeredness, or problems and expect at the same time to feel like rejoicing in the Spirit. Choosing a certain time for being alone, listening to praise music, reading Scripture, and worshiping by thanking God for who He is will help lead us into a time of rejoicing.

Following Christ's public model, we must not let our attention become diverted from the Father—our object of praise. For God's glory we connect with the emotions of Jesus, take on His mind, grow into His image to become one with Him, and produce spiritual fruit. These movements develop as the result of a commitment, accomplished only with Christ through the Holy Spirit.

> "It is only in the man Christ Jesus that such a life is to be seen...His life is our life; He gave Himself for us; He Himself is now our life. The discovery, and the confession, and the denial, of self, as usurping the place of God, of self-seeking and self-trusting, is essential, and yet is what we can not accomplish in our own strength. It is the incoming and indwelling, the Presence and the Rule in the heart, of our Lord Jesus who glorified the Father on earth...who can cast out all self-glorifying, and give us instead His own God-glorifying life and Spirit."[4]

Although Christians have been given authority over the enemy, we are to accent our personal security in Christ Jesus, rejoice in the Holy

Spirit, and praise the Holy Father. Our rejoicing is always to be in the Holy Father, not ever in any power or authority that Christ has given us. One main emotional support that rests under our life's trials is rejoicing in the Lord. Our moral and spiritual condition is a fair test of how we rejoice in the Lord.[5] Our rejoicing is to be accented with the emotional security that our names are written in Heaven. As we rejoice in the Holy Spirit, we speak praise to Holy Father and focus on Him as our praise object.

Examples of Rejoicing and Praising God in Spite of Some Relationships

Rejoicing usually requires work on our part to come to the emotional and mental place of entering into celebration and praise to the Father, especially before others. This is true for some of us, sadly, because many church leaders do not follow Christ's model to rejoice openly in the Holy Spirit. As a child, Sharon experienced this. Even though her mother celebrated the Lord with eagerness, her father as well as the church leaders felt very constrained in this area. In her teenage years, however, they switched to a church where members were encouraged to follow Christ's public model of rejoicing in the Holy Spirit and praising the Father. In some ways, this would prove to be a freeing spiritual experience for Sharon; in other ways, spiritual freedom did not come.

Her father's relationship with his parents in many ways had not been loving. Without realizing this effect on him, her father carried the same attitude into his parenting. Because he believed Sharon should be an example for the younger siblings, undue emotional pressure was placed on her to conform even in her personality. Through the years, this caused much frustration for her since she didn't feel the freedom to develop her God-given personality and abilities under the guidance of Holy Spirit. In childhood, Sharon learned she could get only so close to her father. When she did try to be open with her father he would take advantage of that and heap new guilt on her to conform to his image, rather than Christ's image. He would say things like, "Now that I've got your attention, I want to point out some things you need to be working on."

Since her father's unloving attitude clouded Sharon's picture of our Heavenly Father, in many ways she had come to see Him as unloving. At the same time, she was growing in Christ, developing spiritual gifts, and serving the Lord in many ways. After marriage she felt even more freed-up to develop into the person God intended her to be. With her husband and in the Body of Christ where they worship, Sharon is encouraged to follow Christ's model of praising the Father. For her, the desire to celebrate the Lord comes from within and she expresses this physically through raising her hands, singing, and at times clapping to the music. These expressions come from knowing that she was created to be loved by Christ, to be redeemed, and to be His Bride.

Spiritual and emotional healing continue to enter her life as she tries to keep a constant, deep awareness of God's presence. Sharon says, "I can always tap into the Holy Spirit and feel His presence, joy, and peace. It's like a lake that is calm on the bottom, even though storms may be on top." Recently, God revealed Himself to her in a new way. As Sharon was worshiping the Lord, she felt such an aura of heaviness from God's presence that she had to sit down. Quiet before the Lord, she heard Him say, "I love you." Having experienced a judging criticism from her earthly father, she kept waiting for correction from her Heavenly Father. Again He spoke, "No, I'm not going to correct you. My love is not like any human love you've known. My love is given freely for I never use My love to try to coerce you in any way."

This closeness with God, this loving acceptance without criticism, has given Sharon a new trust for Him. Sharon agrees that we don't rejoice in authority over demons but rejoice in Him. She says, "Not celebrating what we can do, but celebrating who we are in Christ and what we were created to be, is real rejoicing of the Father."

Another woman also has learned to rejoice and praise the Father in spite of a poor relationship. After years of emotional struggles, Lorraine began to see the importance of learning to follow Jesus' model of rejoicing in the Holy Spirit. She grew up in a home life controlled by legalistic attitudes and choices with a strong work ethic. Work provided most of her "good strokes." After Lorraine became a Christian she had difficulty always "feeling" Jesus Christ's love and God's peace. Later she learned about the concept that parents are a child's first picture of God. Her father had been stern and legalistic, sharing few fun times, closeness, or generosity with his family. Consequently, that became Lorraine's picture of God the Father and Jesus the Son.

After marriage, learning to relax and share fun times with her family seemed to be the hardest for Lorraine to learn. Some years ago, she began learning about Christ's model in the sixth chapter of Mark where He took time to relax. Seeing Jesus take out time from a busy, hectic schedule to rest and relax encouraged Lorraine to "see" she could also do the same. Giving consideration to her inner needs began an emotional chain reaction, helping to change Lorraine's mental picture of God the Father and Jesus the Son. She began to view Them as kind, approachable, and fun-loving. This greatly affected Lorraine's prayer life, enabling her to incorporate praise, worship, and a feeling of closeness. These helped her *feel* Jesus' love and God's peace.

After that, Lorraine began feeling emotionally free to relax, rest, and enjoy fun times with her family. Prayer with God the Father and Jesus the Son through Holy Spirit became a time of spiritual enrichment and rejoicing. The church where she worships doesn't encourage members to praise and celebrate the Father openly. But as she keeps God as her praise object, like Jesus did, Lorraine rejoices in the Holy Spirit to celebrate the Father.

Jesus Christ and Praising His Father and Rejoicing

Jesus didn't just "talk the talk"; He "walked the walk" and modeled how to rejoice in the Holy Spirit and give praise to God, our Heavenly Father. Jesus did this by rejoicing greatly in the Holy Spirit saying, "I praise Thee, O Father, Lord of heaven and earth" (Lk. 10:21). It's most significant that this one recorded time of Jesus rejoicing in the Spirit came directly after cautioning His disciples and followers to not accent the devil and demons.

Jesus assured His followers that the most important truth for them to accent and rejoice in was their names being recorded in Heaven. Jesus then showed them how to celebrate and praise the Father. "Rejoice" also describes Abraham's feelings when he saw Jesus and His day (see Jn. 8:56). In His rejoicing, Jesus was also thanking God for His unique way of designing salvation so that even the very young could participate in the security of a personal salvation. This celebrating and praising "was a product in Christ—and therefore in his human nature—of the operations of the Holy Spirit, whom we must suppose to have been always working in the human soul of Christ, sustaining and strengthening it."[6] This picture of Holy Spirit's ministering work in Christ was also a portrait to the disciples for their future spiritual needs in relationships. Jesus modeled for us a clear, practical design of rejoicing in the Holy Spirit and praising God.

First, Christ drew a clear boundary about rejoicing. He told His followers clearly to not rejoice or boast in the fact that evil spirits are subject to us.

Second, Christ placed within the boundary a clear instruction. He stated that "rejoicing" is to be encircled by the truth of our names being recorded in Heaven.

Third, Jesus Christ celebrated and rejoiced exceedingly in the Holy Spirit, our inner-strength connection with Him and God the Father. Jesus spoke praise to God the Father as His object of praise, and focused on Him.[7] Using these movements we can, like Jesus, bow before God the Father in worshipful, adoring praise.

Summarizing Our Thoughts on Jesus and Relationships and Rejoicing

"So what?" So what that Jesus greatly rejoiced in the Holy Spirit and openly gave praise to God? Does His model encourage you, or make you feel frustrated? Would you like to feel more spiritual freedom in worshiping and praising God? Use Christ's model and draw a clear boundary about rejoicing. Do not rejoice in the fact that Christ gave you authority over evil spirits. Rejoice in that your name is being recorded in Heaven. As did Jesus, celebrate and rejoice exceedingly in the Holy Spirit, our inner-strength connection with Him and God the Father. As you speak praise to God, focus on the Holy Father as your object of praise like Jesus did. Living by His models will enable us to love as Christ did and bow before God in worshipful, adoring praise. But we must accept the challenge to discover and connect with Jesus Christ's emotions. Otherwise, His model cannot help us learn to rejoice! In the next chapter we will discover why Christ felt depressed when facing crises.

Chapter Fifteen

Jesus Felt Depressed
in
the Face of Crises

*[Jesus] began to show grief
and distress of mind
and was deeply depressed.*

Matthew 26:37b AMP

"This bread represents My body which will soon be killed. This juice represents My blood which will soon be shed. Let us celebrate this time of crisis with a cautious ceremony as we eat and drink" (Mt. 26:26-29 par.). This last passover supper with Jesus would be talked and retalked in future days. As He talked, His whole person seemed different. And, they wondered, what did He mean that His body would be killed and His blood shed? Breaking into their thoughts, Jesus tenderly told them that a long, awaited secret would be unfolded shortly showing that one of them would betray Him. Horror and disbelief ran quickly from brain to lips. One by one, then as a group, the disciples pledged their love and loyalty to Christ. "I understand and appreciate your pledges; yet, each of you, like scattered sheep, will desert Me tonight." After that it was as though a thick, misty cloud moved over them as they walked. They could not understand what Jesus was trying to convey to them about His death, which now was only hours away. Reaching the Garden entrance, He told some to sit and wait while He, Peter, James, and John participated in prayer. Jesus seemed agitated, He spoke slowly in a low monotone, and His head drooped. It was as though His entire physical, mental, spiritual, and emotional senses were alerting Him that the final preparation time had come.[1]

Facing and Dealing With Depression

When Jesus and His disciples found a suitable place to pray He told them to sit and wait while He went to pray. For encouragement during prayer Jesus took with Him Peter, John, and James. Walking to a secluded place Jesus confided, "I feel depressed, men.[2] In My soul is a heavy sadness and deep grief; I feel like I'm dying from sorrow" (Mt. 26:37-38 par.). Although they were incapable at that time of seeing the whole emotional picture, in the moonlight as Jesus talked they could see His facial expressions. They heard His emotional response of anguish, dejection, and depression. His depression was the same mental anguish or sorrow or dejection that we feel at times.

Today, a large portion of men, women, teenagers, and children feel depression at some level of intensity and for varying lengths of time. Some have called depression the "common cold" of emotional problems. It comes usually without warning and often without apparent cause. Feeling "no hope" to motivate us is one of the main triggers of a depression. We may notice an appetite change; feel agitated; experience a sleeping-pattern change; feel a fatigue or energy loss, a disinterest in daily activities, or an inability to concentrate; have feelings of worthlessness, hopelessness, or sadness; or have thoughts of suicide.[3] When these symptoms cover and control us for at least two weeks, we may feel like our emotional life is being squeezed out. We will need some type of active intervention from family or friends and God, to bring us a motivating hope.

The Reality of Crisis and Depression

Depression not dealt with can create untold misery for those suffering from it as well as their close friends and relatives. Furthermore, many well-meaning Christians try to deny their depression since most relatives do not understand their emotional pain. We hear many give such suggestions as "Just snap out of it" or "Just put your mind on something else." While in the depth of a depression, we have difficulty dealing with even small trials. Actually, "few of us can 'snap out of it'...and every year there are thousands who end their own lives because of it."[4]

Some say in order to better understand depression we need better, clearer ways of describing the various behaviors that manifest depression. Because this has not yet been done, the word *depression* like the word *love* is used to describe a wide range of feelings and experiences. That vagueness adds to the confusion often surrounding this complex emotion, especially in the Christian community. Consequently, we often hear four mistaken ideas repeated about depression. One says that depression is always the result of sin. Another says that depression is caused by a lack of faith in God. A third says that depression is God's face turned against us.

A fourth says that healing from depression is a spiritual exercise.[5] Looking into Christ's various behaviors that showed His suffering from depression can help us turn loose those mistaken ideas about causes of or remedies for depression. Since Scripture tells us Christ suffered from depression, we can see that our feeling depression at times is not out of the ordinary.[6]

Thinking about Christ's emotional suffering when He entered Gethsemane to pray can help us clearly understand His feelings of anguish and sorrow. Awaiting Jesus were three major life losses. He would face extreme bodily suffering (**physical**). We are told that death on a cross is one of the most painful and severe ways of dying. In facing this crisis, Christ knew His body would suffer unspeakably painful torture and shame. Also awaiting Christ was total rejection from His closest friends (**social**). The disciples felt threatened by their loss of personal safety. They also feared the soldiers and hostile multitude who had come to take Jesus. Christ's disciples loved Him, but could not withstand government pressure to conform. They deserted Him, ran, and hid.

The third loss awaiting Christ was separation from His parent, God the Father (**spiritual**). From the sixth hour to the ninth hour, as Christ hung on a cross, total darkness covered the earth and He was separated emotionally from God. He cried out with a loud voice and gave up His spirit. At some point during the next three days, Christ was again separated from communication and fellowship with His Father. We are not sure for how long, but Christ spent some time in "the earth's lower parts" preaching to the spirits in prison. When we consider His major life losses, we see that Christ's feelings of anguish and sorrow were normal for His circumstances.

Different Types and Levels of Depression

Depression comes in different forms and colors, for different reasons, for different lengths of time and levels of severity. Some behaviorists say that if one walks slowly with the head bent forward, speaks in a low monotone or hardly at all, is not very active, or sits with a somewhat huddled posture, we may assume this person may be depressed.[7]

One evening, a handsome and intelligent young man came to my counseling office for an assessment of his emotional state. Several of the above described his behavior, and he seemed to move under a heavy, emotional cloud. In listening to him, I could hear a mental confusion and a strong emotional anxiety. My assessment was that he needed to be connected immediately with a counselor who dealt primarily with depression.

Next day, Ken did see a recommended counselor; however, the following day he committed suicide. Ken evidently felt so confused and overwhelmed in his feelings and thoughts that he could no longer try to, or cared to, cope with reality. Although he attended a church well established in Scripture, he did not know what to do with his emotions of despair and hopelessness. No one had helped him discover and connect with the healthy emotions of Jesus Christ.[8] That's the prescription we all need to help us deal with our losses.

"Losses" are a common reason for depression. Loss of job, loss of security, loss of love, loss of self-esteem, loss of health, or other personal losses can be damaging, destructive, and debilitative to our personhood. Job, naturally, comes to mind when talking of personal loss. He lost everything and everyone, but his life. Talking with his three friends, we can hear Job's anguish. "Let the day of my birth be cursed...and the night when I was conceived. ... Why is a man allowed to be born if God is only going to give him a hopeless life of uselessness and frustration? I cannot eat for sighing; my groans pour out like water" (Job 3:2-3,23-24 TLB). In trying to deal with his losses, Job felt dejection and rejection. These feelings in light of his life crises were normal.

Other Types of Crises and Depression

Other types of life crises may also cause depression. All of us at times suffer from sin, either ours or another's. We feel rejection; we will face death, either ours or that of a loved one. We may face sickness, either ours or another's. King David suffered life crises like trying to deal with the rejection of King Saul, who was out to kill him. David's words reveal his feelings of depression. "How long will You forget me, Lord? Forever? How long will You look the other way when I am in need? How long must I be hiding daily anguish in my heart?...Answer me, O Lord my God; give me light in my darkness lest I die" (Ps. 13:1-3 TLB). At another time in dealing with crisis King David cried out, "My heart is sick; it is trampled like grass and is withered. My food is tasteless, and I have lost my appetite. I am reduced to skin and bones because of all my groaning and despair.... I lie awake, lonely as a solitary sparrow on the roof" (Ps. 102:4-7 TLB). He had lost "hope" that God would deliver him from his crisis. David's feelings of dejection were normal for what he was facing in his life.

While we cannot say King David suffered from a biologically caused depression, the anguish and darkness he "voiced" sound similar to one suffering from brain chemical depletion, which can be caused from ongoing, undealt-with stress. Anyone who has lost hope in suffering from severe depression can relate to King David's feelings of hopelessness and helplessness. Many of us are finding that biological depression is more common than previously acknowledged. One simple suggestion is "that the more serious the depression is in the absence of a recent significant loss, the more likely it is that the cause is biological...and can contribute to the cause of depression in several ways."[9] Also, severe mood swings having to do with our responsiveness toward life adjustments can help trigger a depression experience. King David had not only lived with ongoing stress for many years, but he was trying to deal with severe ongoing life adjustments. His feelings of abandonment, rejection, and depression show he was living with a very low mood swing, which could have been biologically caused.

Further Movement Toward Alleviating Depression

Our brain neurotransmitters are extremely important on the neurochemical and physiological level. They carry impulses between our nerve cells and help regulate behavior having to do with tension, moods, thinking, and alertness. Many of us are beginning to find that we can receive relief from damaging, destructive, and debilitative depression caused from a chemical depletion in the neurotransmitters. Janene had suffered for years from anxiety and mood swings during times of ongoing stress. She especially felt these in winter months when sunshine was scarce. The sun can trigger responses from the brain hormone of melatonin. Janene had also experienced a debilitating depression caused from unresolved issues in her childhood. Since she had resolved most of those issues to experience God's freedom from their control, she knew the difference between the two types of depression.

One friend gave her a quality nutrition book that was written by a medical doctor and his wife, a nutritionist. After reading about chemical depression, Janene decided to use their recommendations and felt immediate relief from the depression and continues to as she uses their suggested vitamin-amino acid replacement therapy.[10] Some of us can diagnose our situation and use the proper replacement therapy required to take care of such depletions.[11] Others, however, can benefit from seeking medical or professional help in determining a depression basis.[12] But regardless of the direction, we need to connect with Jesus Christ's emotions in facing and dealing with depression.

Most counselors have been slow to accept a biological cause for depression. But more are now understanding and treating the results of stress-related depletion in our brain neurotransmitters. It is more complicated and requires more time to deal with since a number of things can go wrong with the neurotransmitters and nerve impulses designed to work together.[13] Counselors must usually cooperate with medical doctors to help clients through medical tests, many just routine, in determining a proper basis for depression.[14] Therefore, they are called on for more "team work." Although it's apparent from Scripture that Christ did not experience a biologically caused depression, many have suffered silently from it for years. Many now understand how undealt-with, ongoing stress can deplete brain neurotransmitters. Those who are using helpful replacement therapy, like Janene, are being set free from the control of that type of depression. Using sound information under the Holy Spirit's guidance can help us, and thousands each year who contemplate suicide, to move away from mental confusion to a peaceful emotional state in our inner being. In the overall picture, becoming connected with Christ's emotions can help us move toward emotional wholeness.

Jesus Christ and Crises and Depression

One common manifestation of depression is turning anger inward on ourselves. When we suffer from depression, we're often afraid to express openly our angry feelings toward the original person who was the source of emotional pain. We fear their retaliation against us and feel helpless against their control over us. We can see from Scripture that Jesus was not angry with God—the source of His emotional pain. Although Matthew talked about Christ suffering from depression, His feelings were not caused by anger towards God or an inward-turned anger.[15] His depression came from anticipating extreme bodily suffering, rejection from all His friends, and separation from His Parent who was waiting for Him.

Submission to God's Divine will in Gethsemane kept Jesus from turning anger in on Himself. In dying for our sin, He placed Himself willingly under God's leadership.[16] "When Jesus set His face to go to Jerusalem it was with a clear view of what should befall Him there—we may even say that it was because He had in a sense decided to die."[17] Regardless of the cost, Christ told His Father He would cooperate to the fullest. His cooperation, however, did not come from a helpless, hopeless, or passive will. His firm will and emotional response to reality show us how to face and deal with depression.

First, Jesus admitted and faced His reality. He did not avoid an indescribably painful death on a cross. Neither did Jesus let His thought process become exaggerated or out of control.

Second, Jesus realized the need for a broader picture of His situation. In prayer He sought God's perspective, His Reliable Source. We don't know the Father's words to Jesus; but, they motivated Him to do God's will.

Third, Jesus replaced His feelings of depression with "hope." God's perspective evidently reminded Jesus that His "death" would save many souls and that His time to return home had come.[18] Because this hope replaced His anguish caused from the upcoming three major life losses, Jesus endured the cross, despising the shame, and sat down at God the Father's right hand.

Summarizing Our Thoughts on Jesus and Crises and Depression

"So what?" So what that Jesus felt depressed in the face of crises? What does that do for you? Are you struggling with depression? Use Christ's practical model. Admit and face your reality; this does not necessarily mean agreeing with it. In facing reality, don't allow your thoughts to become exaggerated or out of control. Admit your need for dealing with depression and choose to not avoid or deny reality. From God's insight and if needed another reliable source, seek a broader perspective on your situation. Use the *perspective* as hope and motivation to keep going. But if you desire Christ's power over depression, you will need to discover and connect with Jesus' emotions! In the next chapter, we will discover why Jesus felt forsaken in facing crises.

Chapter Sixteen

Jesus Felt Forsaken
in
the Face of Crises

My God, My God,
why have You forsaken Me—
deserting Me,
and leaving Me helpless and abandoned?

Mark 15:34b AMP

"My God, My God, why have You forsaken Me?" (Mk. 15:34 AMP) Those intense feelings of abandonment springing from the Sinless One came not from a mild resignation. His was a pain too great to contain so He released it in a shriek of sorrow. When some mocking bystanders heard His shriek they thought He was calling on Elijah before dying. Trying to revive Jesus, one took a sponge filled with sour wine and pushed it in His mouth. Shuddering from shameful exposure and the bitter taste, God's Son again shrieked and surrendered His spirit to the Heavenly Father. A shudder ran through Nature. Rumblings like a powerful freight train filled the air; the trembling ground rattled houses; and rocks forcefully cracked open. Graves opened. A loud ripping noise filled the Temple. God's Mighty Hand was ripping open the 60-foot long, 30-foot wide magnificent drape from top to bottom. It covered the entrance of the Most Holy Place and had taken about 300 priests to manipulate it.[1] With this heavy drape gone, the Most Holy Place, where animal blood sacrifices were made for sin, was thrown open forever. This signified that cleansing for sin could come only from Christ's shed-blood sacrifice. It meant everyone had open access to Almighty God, no longer having to go through a high priest. We approach God in prayer through the Holy Spirit. With Christ's mission complete, He was emotionally reconnected to His Holy Father.[2]

Handling the Feeling of Being Forsaken

There are differences of opinion as to why Christ felt forsaken by the Father.[3] One thought says that His feeling of abandonment enabled Him to identify with others who also feel abandoned by God. On the flip side, though, Christ's death is viewed as a failure, leaving the poor in their suffering and struggle for justice.[4] Another, says Christ felt abandonment because He had become sin for us and the Father could not look on sin.[5] A third, says the Father's hatred for sin was directed personally onto Christ, "so that in his own heart he felt what it meant to be opposed by heaven, having the breath of an angry God on him."[6]

While the first view cannot be substantiated from Scripture, the second and third fail to consider the Holy Father's love for His only begotton Son. "The Son, who from everlasting was the object of the Father's supreme pleasure, empirically felt what it meant to have that fellowship cut"[7] when God asked Him—the only begotten, sinless Son—to become sin for you and me. As Jesus became our sin, the Father's great love for that precious Son made it impossible for Him to look on Christ's suffering. That is why Jesus felt God's emotional abandonment and shrieked, "My Father, why didn't You help Me? Why did You forsake Me?" Jesus is the only qualified One who can show us how to face and handle the feeling of abandonment.

The Reality of Crises and Being Forsaken

Losing the Father's intimate fellowship and approval at death's door filled Christ with the infinite, indescribable emotional pain of being forsaken. His emotional pain is the same as today when we feel abandoned or deserted or left helpless. Those feelings describe Christ's last recorded emotions as He died. Earlier, Christ spoke about His and God's oneness in relationship and "equality" in which They shared all things. He called God His Father, life model, work model, teacher, and motivator. Jesus said God loved Him, gave all judgment to Him, and gave Him authority to execute judgment. Christ said that He did not seek His own will, but God's will; He said His works not only bear witness of Him but show that the Father had sent Him. Losing such unique oneness and closeness was unbearable. "My Father God, why did You forsake Me," was a normal response.

We're not told *how* God broke the connection between them; but His temporary withdrawal sent shock waves through the God-man's emotions. Because of the "oneness" they shared, Christ knew instantly when

His Father could no longer look on Him for fellowship and communion. There's no greater emotional pain than abandonment, or perceived abandonment, by a loved one. Terry has felt forsaken emotionally by her mother since she was a young child. Her mother lost two children through miscarriage and crib death; she gave birth to Terry's older sister just eleven months before Terry was born. Added to that, Terry's father was an alcoholic. Trying to cope with all those losses and frustrations created a collected anger within her mother about everything in life. This anger usually spewed onto Terry, the innocent bystander, several times each day leaving her without protection or safety.

Terry's feelings of being forsaken emotionally heightened at age ten when her mother divorced her father. Although he suffered from alcohol abuse and died when Terry was 15, she remembers him as kind and compassionate in comparison to her mother. When Terry was 13, her mother remarried—which opened the door to a different dynamic. Her new stepfather, also an alcoholic, started crossing Terry's privacy boundaries. Even though she complained, her mother would not assume the responsibility of believing or protecting. At age 16, wanting to be believed and feel respected, Terry took her stepfather to court. Even then the mother refused to stand with Terry and called her a liar. The court placed Terry in a girl's home, which made her feel like a criminal rather than the one who had been betrayed and abused. Twenty years later, Terry would like to feel close to her mother. But she remains cold and distant, refusing to admit the abuse was real. This still causes Terry to feel abandoned emotionally, which is a form of emotional death.

Understanding Crises and Feeling Forsaken

Gaining a clear understanding of God's sovereignty is important in trying to handle feelings of abandonment. If we "see" God as cruel, overbearing, or cold, we won't be able to trust Him with life's circumstances. Because God knows what's best for us, He has the "right to deal with his creatures just as seems good in his sight."[8] Even when we don't understand His ways, His way will ultimately prove best for us. This is hard to accept during those times when we feel we cannot crawl through another day. Our acceptance determines whether or not we exalt God as "head above all" and cooperate with Him as He "causes all things to work together for good to those who love God" (Rom. 8:28). This "causing" can be very hard to accept. Feeling abandoned, desperately we cry out, "Why God, why me? Where are You? Why don't You help me?"

In dealing with God's "right" we must remember that God not only works through love, He **is** love. He also is all knowing (omniscient), all powerful (omnipotent), and everywhere present (omnipresent). God is the all-trustworthy one; He never changes; and God is Holy. He does not pervert good for evil or evil for good. The experiences God allows are often painful. Yet, through His omniscience and Holiness He knows when "what" is best for us. Also, He walks with us through the "what"; He never leaves nor forsakes us.[9] When we come to terms with *who* God is, then we begin to "see" that God's sovereignty is acceptable. King David did that. He said, "As for God, His way is perfect!" (Ps. 18:30 AMP) We do not travel this road alone. Through God's omniscient right in our lives we have His power through Holy Spirit to help us discover, study, and connect with the emotions of Jesus—the Jesus we can know and love.

Jesus Christ and Crises and Feeling Forsaken

Christ's way of handling crises and abandonment is a practical model for us in dealing with feeling forsaken and clinging to a personal faith in God's sovereignty and power. "Our Lord's great object in laying down His life upon the cross was the Father's glory. No other object was worthy of Him"[10] That pain-filled cry of "My God, My God" models His faith and trust in His Heavenly Father during the most difficult, trying, hard-to-understand situation. Christ the Son was expressing His confidence in God the Father who was turning defeat into conquest. Even death could not change the Divine reality of Father and Son teaming together.

Jesus Christ agreed to death on a cross in order to purchase salvation for all of mankind—regardless of race, age, or gender. Yet, Christ's suffering for the glory of God and not for self or vain glory became His *joy*. "In His extreme agonies our Lord Jesus placed this joy before Him, and consoled Himself by foreseeing that God would be praised by seeking souls in consequence of His death."[11] Christ believed that God had a reason for asking Him to suffer indescribable pain. Souls, plucked from the devil, would live forever with Them in Heaven. Satan and his "dark angels" did not win; God had brought conquest out of defeat. We can never fully describe Christ's emotion of feeling forsaken by the Heavenly Father. However, we can dwell on and incorporate into our lives His practical, applicable behavior model.

First, Jesus stayed with the conflict. He could have refused the cross or called ten thousand angels to His defense. He did neither. Jesus walked through the experience of death to His human self-will.

Second, Christ endured others' insults and abusiveness for a season. This in itself is not why He came to earth; therefore, that did not become a way of life for Him. While Christ did not excuse the abusive behavior, He did suffer their wrongs for a season in order to do God's Divine will.

Third, Christ faced the reality of God's abandonment. He did this by expressing, rather than denying, His emotional pain of separation from His Parent. Then, regardless of cost, Christ clung to faith in God's sovereignty and power which motivated Him to keep going.[12] That is Christ's model for us when we need to handle the pain of feeling emotionally forsaken.

Summarizing Our Thoughts on Jesus and Crises and Feeling Forsaken

"So what?" So what that Jesus Christ felt forsaken in facing crises? What does that do for you? Have you ever felt forsaken? Like Christ, you can stay in the conflict and not run because of emotional pain. Like Christ, you can endure others' hostility for a season; but do not allow that to become a way of life. We are to live as overcomers, not victims. Like Christ, you can face your reality of feeling forsaken and in the midst of it express emotional pain rather than deny your hurt. This can help you cling to faith and trust in God's sovereignty. For unless you accept the challenge to discover and connect with Jesus' emotions, His models cannot help you! In the next chapter we will discover why Jesus felt troubled while facing crises.

Chapter Seventeen

Jesus Felt Troubled
in
the Face of Crises

He was deeply moved in spirit
and troubled—
He chafed in spirit,
and sighed and was disturbed.

John 11:33b AMP

"I have glorified Thy name, and I will glorify it again" (Jn. 12:28 par.). To some of the crowd there with Jesus, God's mighty voice had sounded like thunder. The rest, however, felt convinced that an angel spoke to Jesus. He had been telling the Father that His insides were stirred up like waters in the Bethesda pool. His soul was troubled; He felt restless and agitated. On the one hand His flesh was crying, "Father, save Me from this hour [of trial and agony]" (Jn. 12:27 AMP). On the other hand, Jesus' mind argued that He had come to earth for the very purpose of suffering and dying on a cross. His inner cry was, "Holy Father, glorify Thy name!" When God answered, Christ didn't try to clarify where the voice came from. He merely explained that the "voice" had spoken for their benefit and not His. Then Jesus explained further that the time had come for the evil genius of this world to be cast out. He drew a mental picture about His very soon death. Jesus said when He is lifted up on a cross all men, Gentile as well as Jew, would be drawn to Him. With their spiritual eyes still unlightened they could not "see" His picture. Since it was not yet Christ's hour, He departed and hid Himself from them for a while. Jesus was needing space and time to help Him cope with a troubled soul.[1]

Coping With a Troubled Soul

When our feelings cause us inward commotion and agitation, taking away our calmness of mind, we feel troubled.[2] The reasons for feeling troubled in facing crises come in different shapes, shades, and sizes. In three different situations involving the disciples, Christ had to cope with His and others' troubled emotions. Christ's blunt, unexpected statement about Lazarus' death shocked the disciples, and they reacted with troubled emotions. They felt further troubled when Jesus announced His intentions to return to Judea to see Lazarus. They believed that would be fatal for Him. When struggling with the cross crisis, Jesus felt troubled in His soul. Later, in talking with the disciples about His very soon death and the fact that one of them would betray Him, He felt troubled in spirit. They felt equally troubled as they tried to cope with their shock over which one would betray Christ. Coping with situations that cause us inner agitation, taking away calmness of mind, produces emotionally troubled souls.

The Reality of Crises and a Troubled Soul

Feeling great emotional pain, Martha was accusing Jesus of failing her by not being there when her brother died. Her reprimand went over Christ's head, and with loving concern He assured her that Lazarus would again live if she believed. When she affirmed her belief in the resurrection, He responded, "I am the resurrection and the life; he who believes in Me shall live even if he dies, and everyone who lives and believes in Me shall never die. Do you believe this?" (Jn. 11:25-26) Martha told Jesus that she believed, then left to find Mary. When the two sisters and their friends returned, they saw Jesus weeping. This caused them mixed feelings; some sympathized, while others criticized. But after listening to Jesus talk about His feelings, they realized that Christ's tears flowed from a righteous anger at the distress into which enemy death had plunged them.[3]

This was an awesome moment. Christ was trying to demonstrate to them God's power, but their spiritual eyes were heavy. They could not "see" that in only moments Lazarus would get up and walk. As a result, instead of cooperating to roll away the gravestone, they resisted through disbelief. This "disbelief" coming from the ones who were very significant to Jesus—those into whom He had poured His life—was more than He could tolerate. Facing the crisis of Lazarus' death was like facing the death of a close family member. Jesus "groaned with the sisters in deep emotion, emotion out of which an involuntary cry was wrung from his heart," a troubled heart.[4]

Another Example of Feeling Troubled Emotions

Each of us has experienced different degrees of a troubled soul from inward commotion that causes us to lose our calmness of mind when facing a crisis. Some years ago, Jane shared with me an experience that caused her inner agitation during a difficult decision time. She and two other young ladies were given the opportunity to leave their jobs in Oklahoma City and move to New York City for a year. The reason for their move was to become members of the Greater New York Billy Graham Crusade office staff. They were to ask their employer, pastor, and parents for letters of recommendation and approval. All had been obtained, except the one from Jane's parents. She had travelled 200 miles for their letter only to find that her father felt her living in the large city would be too dangerous. Jane's mother wanted her to go, but did not feel free to go against the father's position.

Jane returned to Oklahoma City thinking that her other friends would have to travel to New York without her. However, the woman responsible for that decision said Jane could go and work in the New York crusade office. Two weeks later, she again visited her parents to say good-bye. The reality of leaving her family, present job, and friends to move to the large city began causing second thoughts. Feeling inner agitation and great mental anxiety, she walked a short distance to the small town's old iron bridge. On that warm summer day the sky held many large, beautiful, white cotton-candy-like clouds. Walking toward the bridge, Jane was arguing with God about all the reasons why she should not leave. She was describing how much better her service would be there, than in the large city.

Several feet from the old bridge she heard a booming thunder from the sky which seemed to vibrate over her head. Jane stopped and looked up; the sun was shining brightly, enhancing the cotton-candy-like clouds. She heard a loud inner voice say, "Get back to the house, get ready to go, and stop rebelling." Jane believed that was God's angry voice reprimanding her and headed back immediately for her parent's house. She asked if anyone had heard thunder; the answer was "no." Only she had heard the booming noise God had used to get her attention. In submitting to and obeying the Lord God, her inner agitation and great mental disturbance ended. All details fit together, and about one week later the three young ladies arrived in New York City. Jane spent a challenging, rewarding, and safe year of service to the Lord Jesus. During that year is when I also joined the Crusade office staff and met Jane.

Jesus Christ and Crises and Feeling Troubled

Falling on her knees Mary accused, "Lord, if You had been here, my brother would not have died" (Jn. 11:32). This last reprimand was the final straw to fall onto Christ's emotional haystack. For many days He had given everything emotionally, spiritually, mentally, and physically. He felt very vulnerable. He had depleted Himself by trying to prepare His disciples for Lazarus' death and resurrection. But they, at that time having nothing with which to compare Christ's words, couldn't understand. Martha, Mary, and their Jewish friends were also unable to understand and wept together. The one they loved so deeply not only was dead but after four days, "he stinketh."

All together, it was too much. The crisis of Lazarus' death, for Christ, was more than just the idea of death; He was thinking about something beyond the physical aspect of death. Behind death Christ "saw Him who has the power of death, and that sin which constitutes the sting of death…His whole being revolted" in anger and repugnance to what death does to the **life** of His precious created beings.[5] The sound of Mary, Martha, and their friends wailing over Lazarus' dead body caused Jesus to feel deeply moved in spirit and troubled, bringing Him to tears (see Jn. 11:29-35).

When Christ was facing His own death, He said, "My soul has become troubled" (Jn. 12:27). Christ knew the true agony of a troubled soul. Because of facing crises, "He understands the grief which troubles your fainting heart, and enters into all your distresses while you are bewailing yourself and lamenting that you cry in the daytime and the Lord hears not, and that in the night season you plead in vain."[6] In facing His crises rather than running, Jesus understands when we feel troubled. For instance, when Jesus faced the crisis of coping with God's "right" to end Lazarus' life, Jesus believed God made His decision for the ultimate good of all involved. By working through His troubled crises, Jesus modeled for us how to face and deal with crises.

First, Jesus showed how He felt emotionally in a particular situation. He didn't try to squelch either His or others' feelings. Jesus was open and vulnerable with the truth that He felt troubled in soul.

Second, Jesus took control of the situation to bring forth good for as many as possible. He did not dwell on His own needs; however, He displayed clearly His righteous anger at the distress into which death had plunged family and friends.

Third, Jesus exercised faith in God and challenged others to do so as well. Even in His time of troubled emotions, He asked those involved to exercise faith and obedience. He praised God in prayer and finished His commitment to bring closure to the situation.[7] Christ's model of facing and coping with a troubled soul can be helpful to us if we will but follow it during crises.

Summarizing Our Thoughts on Jesus and Crises and Feeling Troubled

"So what?" So what that Jesus felt troubled in facing crises? How do you typically try to cope with a troubled soul? Do you succeed? Follow Jesus' model and learn to express your emotions in a healthy way (rather than squelch them) when troubled. Like Christ, we can try to change a situation to bring about good for as many as possible. In trying to bring closure to a situation, like Christ, we can choose to exercise faith in God the Father and praise Him for His faithfulness. But it's up to us to discover and connect with Jesus' emotions, and follow His model in coping when feeling troubled! In the following chapter, we will discover why Jesus cried and shed tears when facing crises.

Chapter Eighteen

Jesus Cried and Shed Tears
in
the Face of Crises

In the days of His flesh,
[Jesus] offered up both prayers and supplications
with loud crying and tears
to the One able to save Him from death....

Hebrews 5:7

"Rabbi, the Jews only recently tried to stone You; why do You want to go back to their territory?" (Jn. 11:8 par.) Concern for Christ's safety jumped from the disciples' lips as He spoke of returning to Judea. Jesus responded "that duty, not safety, was His first obligation."[1] He reminded them of the 12 hours of daylight with which they could journey faster and safer. After arriving at Bethany and giving physical life back to Lazarus, Jesus was honored with a special dinner at Simon the leper's home. While they were eating, a woman came and anointed Jesus' head and feet with a very expensive perfume. Several felt offended by the woman's actions, especially Judas Iscariot, and accused her of being wasteful. Satan was urging the heart of Judas to do his **worst** toward Christ, while the Holy Spirit was moving Mary's heart to pour out her *greatest* for Christ. Jesus defended Mary's act of loving honor as anointing His body for burial.[2] He was trying to provide them with a picture of the horrendous pain that awaited Him. Just thinking about the pain caused Him to offer prayers with loud cries and tears.[3]

Feeling the Need for Crying and Shedding Tears

Wailing in distress and shedding tears aren't always just in connection with some personal need. Feeling the need to cry often comes when we see another's pain and want to meet that need. This is true more particularly when the one we are trying to help is a family member or close friend. "The misfortune, even the slight misfortune, of a dear friend stirs us much more powerfully than the greater calamity of one with whom we have no special tie."[4] We see this to some degree with Jesus. He is known as being moved often with compassion, but only a few times does Scripture state that He cried and shed tears.[5] One time, over His city of Jerusalem (see Mt. 23:37; Lk. 19:41); once, at His friend Lazarus' grave (see Jn. 11:34-35); and at times, in His praying (see Heb. 5:7). In each of these circumstances, Christ's concern was for others rather than for Himself.

The Reality of Crying and Shedding Tears

In each instance where Jesus was wailing in distress and shedding tears, it was because of His sensitive vulnerability toward others. Christ gave these "appropriate for the occasion" models of crying and shedding tears for everyone, women or men, to follow even in public. To the opposite in our society, crying and tears from men or boys are often frowned upon and made fun of as being *sissy*. Before kindergarten most little boys begin to hear from parents or other adults that "crying is for babies." So even if they fall and skin a knee or are hit by someone, many little boys learn early to not cry. Instead, they stuff their emotional pain. Resulting from this shame-based discipline, these boys build up hostility. They learn that healthy emotions are neither relevant nor important. These confusing, shaming lies go with men into adulthood where a large percent spew collected hostility onto innocent wives and children, which frustrates and shames their relationships.

Although Scripture does not give clear specifics, we have sufficient details about Jesus' everyday life to know that collected hostility does not describe Him. Others felt drawn to Jesus because of His outgoing way of relating. The New Testament records over 30 different emotions that Jesus responded through, appropriate for the occasion. He worked, lived, and associated quite closely for three years with 12 men plus many friends—including women and children. His effect on them was such that they committed their lives to serving Him. While Jesus was straightforward with them, He related through love, respect, kindness, and fairness, which are the opposite of shame.

One Example of Feeling Shame and Shedding Tears

Few escape being shamed as children. Dennis did not; when he was only three, his mother died. For many years he was bounced from one foster home to another, suffering extreme emotional abuse. Dennis shed many tears. Because of the insecurity, cruelty, and instability from his living situations, at age four he still sometimes lost bladder control. Those in charge of him decided he should be punished by having to wear diapers. That day, friends came to visit his foster parents. Dennis felt shamed about having to wear a diaper and hid behind the couch. But the foster parents pulled him out, wearing only a diaper, and made Dennis stand before the adults while they ridiculed and made fun. In his adulthood, Dennis still suffers scars from that shame-based authority and lack of healthy sensitivity for his emotional needs.

Many little boys turn to competition for fulfillment, lacking closeness with a father and an adequate role model of genuine manhood. Sports, grades, music, drugs, illicit sex, conversations; in whatever they do, most try to be number one. Added to this imbalance, "Parents often compare the personal achievements of their sons with the accomplishments of other boys. A boy learns that other boys, and later other men, are his competitors and, therefore, potential enemies."[6] This type of confused, off-balanced thinking undermines most little boys' ability to build friendships with each other. Carrying that thinking over into adulthood emotionally hampers them in their relationships. Some say, "The American male is lonely and friendless, but must maintain his macho image at all costs, even if it means isolation from people."[7] For most American males, isolation is usually where they cry and shed tears.

Jesus Christ and Crying and Shedding Tears

Christ did not isolate Himself from people **or** crying **or** shedding tears. Hebrews says Jesus cried loudly and shed tears while praying and talking with His Father. Luke says Christ cried over His city of Jerusalem. John says that Jesus openly cried at Lazarus' tomb. "The sight of the distress into which death had plunged Mary and her companions" threw Christ into an inward agitation.[8] In facing His own death, Jesus realized in a most powerful and disquieting way what death meant for others. He did not deny or stuff His feelings; His emotional responses were sincere. His tears were "the swift spontaneous outburst of the warmest tenderness of human emotion...the outpouring of a Divine compassion."[9] Even today, Jesus does not isolate Himself; He feels for and with others in pain through us, His family.

Whether in private or in public, we can believe God did not see Christ's crying as shameful. God heard Jesus because of His piety or reverence; He didn't shame Jesus for His emotions. God's approval gave Jesus the courage to openly express His healthy and appropriate emotions. The loud crying and shedding tears from Christ were acceptable to God. This acceptance gave Him encouragement and nurtured His manhood. Christ, the Perfect Personality, modeled how to be open and vulnerable in facing relational crises.

First, Christ did not praise or exalt Himself. We don't see in Him a self-centered, off-balanced, emotionally hampered person. Just the opposite. Christ showed us how to be genuine and balanced in each area of life.

Second, Christ released tension unashamedly through loud crying and shedding tears. Whenever a situation presented the need for an emotional response, His emotional responses were appropriately expressed.

Third, Christ saw life as an opportunity to learn self-control. He modeled and lived servanthood. Being open, honest, and appropriate with His emotional responses helped Christ release tension in healthy ways.[10] This eliminated the buildup of any damaging anger collection and enabled the God-man to live with emotional balance.

Summarizing Our Thoughts on Jesus and Facing Crises and the Need to Cry

"So what?" So what that Jesus cried and shed tears in facing crises? What does that do for you? When you feel the need to cry, do you squelch that need in shame? If so, you can learn from Christ's openness. Like Christ, you must avoid praising or exalting yourself. He kept an emotionally balanced responsiveness. When appropriate, as Christ did, you can unashamedly release tension through crying and tears when facing crises, even in public. Like Christ, you can learn self-control and develop a servant's heart for Jesus' sake. But it's your responsibility to discover and connect with Jesus' emotions, using His model to help you face crises! In the following chapter we will discover why Jesus felt anger over others' sin.

Chapter Nineteen

Jesus Felt Anger
Over
Others' Sin

...Is it lawful and right on the Sabbath to do good
or to do evil, to save life or to take it?
But they kept silence. And
He glanced around at them with vexation and anger....

Mark 3:4-5 AMP

"Out! Out! My House is a place of prayer; but you are trying to make it into a den of thieving tradesmen!" (Mk. 11:17 par.) As Christ whipped a scourge of cords in the air, loud snaps echoed across the inner Temple. Overturned tables left behind startled, disbelieving moneyhandlers. In one split second, dumped coins clanked on the cold cobblestone and drowned the traders' hawking voices. Chairs flew over shocked and flattened traders, sprawling on the floor. Plopping of hard sandals filled the air as legs bounded to the courtyard. Between breaths Jesus was muttering something like, "These stubborn and hard-hearted people never seem to learn. They know this is a House of worship. Yet, they defiantly came in here and defiled my House by selling doves and animals." Jesus gave us a rightly directed anger model when He cleansed His sacred place. After clearing the Temple of congestion and noise, Jesus restored it to a place of prayer. As blind and lame came to Jesus, He healed them and grateful children sang praises to Him. This infuriated the chief priests and they railed in indignation against Christ. After answering their accusations, He went out of the city for rest. Even though Scripture does not say Jesus acted out of anger in the Temple, it's hard to visualize the above without describing it as angry behavior in action.[1]

Handling Anger When Dealing With Others' Emotional Hardness

Anger is one of the most commonly and most often recorded emotional responses from Christ. Since Scripture says Jesus Christ the God-man felt and responded with anger, we can believe His anger responses were healthy and appropriate. There are ten New Testament words that express anger, but Christ only expressed three of those. His expressions of anger were in response to dealing with others' sin. For example, in a synagogue one Sabbath Christ saw the shriveled hand of a man and wanted to heal him. He also saw some Pharisees watching, looking for a reason to accuse Him. Their legalistic view of not healing on the Sabbath was more important to them than the man's need to be healed.

Jesus gave the Pharisees opportunity to agree with Him that the shriveled hand needed healing, but they remained silent. When they refused to agree with Him for the man's healing, He looked around at them with the type of anger or wrath we feel in reaction against what gives us discomfort.[2] Christ did not deny His feelings; He felt very discomforted with the Pharisees' lack of compassion. Against their hardened hearts, Christ displayed a balanced and appropriate anger.

The Reality of Anger

We hear differing opinions regarding anger's origination. Some say anger is learned and others say we're born with it. One view says we typically feel anger as an "almost automatic inner response" of frustration or fear when we are hurt by someone.[3] Others declare anger to be one of the "authentic" or "real" feelings in that it is a response that can help us "deal with a specific set of circumstances."[4] One helpful description sees anger as a physical state of readiness or preparedness to help us in the defense of life situations. In that sense, anger could be called a physiological energizer.[5] Surrounding these differing opinions, I hold the view that each of us possesses a God-given "anger capacity" from which we daily feel and express different forms of anger. The challenge is learning to feel and express healthy, balanced, and appropriate anger as did Christ over others' sin or hardness of heart.

One Example of Heart Hardness

Have you ever had to deal with someone's hardness of heart? Lawrence did. His father had called him so many curse words he hardly recognized, "Lawrence." Added to that humiliation, his father controlled by alcohol would beat him over the slightest irritation. When I became acquainted with Lawrence in his early twenties, he was having difficulty getting and holding a job. Although Lawrence was an intelligent and likeable young man, his head was filled with deceptions about who he was as a person. His self-identity was very fuzzy and his self-esteem feelings sat on zero.

Lawrence believed he was a Christian, but peace or confidence or motivation did not dwell in his mind or will. He was unable to function as an emotionally whole individual, taking responsibility for his everyday life. His good emotions were frozen and he was emotionally stuck in fear and unproductivity. As an adult, he could have benefited from using Christ's model of expressing a healthy anger toward his father. Then he could have allowed a mature Christian to help him walk through the forgiveness process. At that time, however, hate and fear controlled him because of the lack of a healthy parental love and not being connected with Christ's emotions.

Christians and Feeling Anger

Sometimes we need the expression of a healthy anger to protect us from others' attacks or lies or vindictiveness. There are many times and ways where we will meet those with hardened hearts. Rightly directed anger is basically the emotion which prepares us to act in defense of life and integrity. Many Christians have a fuzzy picture of Christ's healthy emotions. They wrongly teach that Jesus was a meek, mild, milk-toast man without integrity. They say all anger is sin and should be denied, squelched, or repressed; but according to Christ's model, anger in itself is not sin. We see this in Christ's balanced behavior at the Temple. He was protecting His "house of prayer" from vindictive tradesmen who had with their evil decisions defiled the Lord's House.

Yet, it's important to note that Christ's behavior was not aggression. Many of us at times confuse aggression with assertiveness, but they aren't the same. "Aggression is unhealthy behavior, having to do with hostility and transgressing on other's rights or responsibilities."[6] We act with aggression when we "trample" on others. On the flip side, "Assertiveness is a healthy behavior, having to do with our affirming or exercising rights and responsibilities."[7] Christ took on the responsibility of clearing out evil from His House of Prayer by using healthy assertiveness. His assertiveness was acting positively in a judgment call, and He had the right to do so. We, too, can use assertive judgment calls in expressing a healthy and rightly directed anger. This gives energy to act responsibly in relation to whatever is wrong or whatever has given us discomfort.

Jesus Christ and Feeling Anger

Christ modeled in balanced and appropriate ways how we can handle feelings of anger. He addressed satan and threatened demons angrily; He was angered by the disease of leprosy. Jesus modeled anger when He turned over the money changers' tables and cleared the Temple of sellers.[8] When Christ felt and expressed anger, His feelings and responses were always appropriate to the occasion. Hardness from the Pharisees' sinful hearts would have kept the crippled man subject to their cruelty. In dealing with their coldness, Christ bypassed them and healed the man's crippled hand. This set the man physically free so he could become productive financially to provide for himself. This angered the Pharisees; they "went out and immediately began taking counsel with the Herodians against Him" (Mk. 3:6). Although we follow Christ's model, we're not guaranteed that others will soften their hardened hearts and change their offensive behavior. If the offender refuses to turn from his hard heart, we may like Christ have to refuse further association with that one. If the offending person is a Christian, we may need to involve other Christians in order to settle the matter. By expressing a healthy and appropriate anger, Christ gave us a practical and useful example to follow so we can learn to rightly direct our expressions of anger.

First, Christ acknowledged the Pharisees' hardness of heart. He didn't excuse them or deny their sin. Jesus expressed anger equal to and appropriate for the sin. Even though His was a strong anger, He was in control of those emotions.

Second, Christ did not pretend their sin was okay. He expressed His feelings of anger over their refusal to relate in a kind, thoughtful way. His strong emotions of anger were in balance with the degree of the Pharisees' sin.

Third, Christ chose a productive solution. He did not let others' sin control or inhibit Him. Choosing what was best overall, Jesus healed the man and set him free. He did not continue to associate with the Pharisees.[9]

Although Christ acknowledged the Pharisees' hard hearts, handled His anger, and chose a productive solution, they did not change their hard hearts. And some of our offenders may not change. Nevertheless, we can follow Christ's model and learn to handle "our" anger in dealing with others' hardness of heart.

Summarizing Our Thoughts on Jesus Christ and Anger Over Others' Sin

"So what?" So what that Jesus felt angry over others' sins? What does that do for you? Do you struggle with controlling anger or expressing healthy anger? Try using Christ's model. Like Christ, you can acknowledge the person's hardness of heart that caused your hurt; you need not excuse or deny the sin. Like Christ, you can express your feelings of anger over the person's refusal to relate in a kind, compassionate way. You need not pretend the sin was okay. Like Christ, you can choose a productive solution; you need not let others' sin control or inhibit you. However, you must accept the challenge of discovering and connecting with Jesus Christ's emotions or His model cannot help you in dealing with anger. In the next chapter we will discover why Jesus felt angry indignation over others' sin.

Chapter Twenty

Jesus Felt the Anger of Indignation Over Others' Sin

...[Jesus] was indignant and pained,
and said to them,
Allow the children to come to Me—
do not forbid or prevent or hinder them—
for to such belongs the kingdom of God.

Mark 10:14 AMP

"If you want to enter My kingdom, you'll have to lay down your pride and become like this little child before you" (Mt. 18:3 par.). After walking with the Perfect Personality for almost three years, the disciples' spiritual maturity was still up for grabs. They were batting words around from one to another and then to Jesus. As a group they asked Jesus who would be the greatest in Heaven, hoping to settle the question of what status awaited them. Pitching a strike three against their arrogance, Jesus told His disciples to lay down their pride if they expected to see Heaven. Jesus explained further that not only are adults to take on humility as a child, but we are to accept children as He does. Christ loves, values, respects, protects, and provides for children. When we do not relate to children in these ways, we are in essence becoming a stumbling block to them. Jesus told His disciples that one would be better off to hang a heavy millstone around the neck and drown in the sea rather than to in any way hinder a child. Then, in indignation, He reprimanded them for their disrespect to children.[1]

Expressing Indignation Over Others' Sin of Disrespect

Christ's indignation is the same displeasure or outrage we feel toward that which seems unjust.[2] Christ's expressions spilled out when His disciples treated little children with disrespect and lack of dignity. Christ's indignation over children being mistreated is most significant. As a whole Body, Christians have failed to express displeasure and outrage at the disrespect shown and the loss of dignity caused by child abuse. We have failed to follow Christ's healthy and appropriate example of indignation (see Mk. 10:13-16). Rampant child abuse and abortion in our communities today call forth indignant outrage from all who love, respect, and accept children as God's gifts of life. Sadly, large portions of the Body of Christ have remained silent on these two sources of evil.

The Reality of Indignation Over Others' Sin

Many Christians openly and privately hold back from expressing their displeasure and outrage over child mistreatment and abortion. Such passive behavior may stem from a belief that "feeling anger" is sinful. We must remember that the emotion of anger is neutral. This emotion cannot be considered either sinful or holy; wrong or right; inappropriate or appropriate. What we do individually with our feelings of anger is what determines whether or not it becomes one of the above. We must judge our anger responses of intensity on the basis of each situation. "In some cases we may actually be sinning by only being mildly irritated when it may be God's will for us to be very angry."[3] With outrage Christ said, "Stop what you're doing to those little children and let them come to Me for My blessings. My kingdom is made of such sweet innocence" (Mk. 10:14-15 par.).

Many women and men who've suffered the base and unjust violations of sexual, verbal, or physical abuse have come to me for counseling. Most suffered the evil disrespect to their personhood as children. Because of this evil disrespect of humanity, survivors usually have a difficult time coming to Christ for His blessings of acceptance, love, and salvation. Yet, they need Christ's healing touch in order to cope with everyday life without their rightful feelings of indignation turning into bitterness. That type of anger produces a bitter taste in our stomach because of a painful experience.[4] All of us at times have to work hard to keep our indignation from turning into the anger feelings of exasperation, where someone provokes us to anger.[5]

Christ **did not** experience these types of anger. Bitterness comes as a result of not obeying the Scriptural instruction: Do not let the sun go down while you are still angry. This means we're not to ignore or deny our anger; rather, we're to seek a helpful resolution. When we stuff anger, deny anger, dilute anger, or freeze anger, our feelings of anger actually progress.

The progression feels like a bitter taste, which invades the stomach and spreads over our entire emotions. We then develop a short anger fuse and the least irritation can set us off. Bitterness, criticalness, and selfishness progressively become a way of life until nothing or no one can make us happy. At that point we're not handling or controlling anger. The anger is progressively controlling us.

One Example of Anger Progression

One Old Testament example of anger progressing into bitterness comes from Cain and Abel. God had instructed Adam, Eve, and their family on the how-to's of bringing sacrificial offerings. Yet, instead of following God's instructions Cain did offerings his way. Consequently, "for Cain and his offering God had no respect or regard. So Cain became exceedingly angry and indignant, and he looked sad and depressed" (Gen. 4:5 par.). While God was the most significant person in Cain's life, he also knew of Adam and Eve's deserved expulsion from the Garden. Thus, Cain may have feared a similar reaction from God. That may have kept him from approaching God for His clarification of why He refused the offering. Yet, Cain could have been helped to work through his anger by choosing a healthy "clearing of the air" interaction with God.

Believers and Lack of Emotional Control

In our present "cult of self" society, for one to admit an out-of-control behavior is at times difficult even for Believers. Like for Cain and Rachel of the Old Testament, the two anger areas of bitterness and exasperation cause many of us to struggle. Cain got into trouble from diluting his anger by pretending that his sacrificial offering was as acceptable as Abel's. Instead of admitting to God his **sinful** failure to obey, Cain instead became very angry with Him. But being angry with such a powerful force seemed too scary for Cain, so he "misplaced" his anger from God onto Abel. By that time, Cain's anger was so strong he could no longer control it. His uncontrolled anger progressed quickly to the depression that comes from turning anger inward on self.

I believe God understood Cain's depressed state of mind filled with self-anger, or even hatred, for what he had done. Since God understood that Cain feared coming, He went to him. God asked, "Why are you angry? And why do you look sad and dejected?" (Gen. 4:6 AMP) We don't know Cain's response, but we have his recorded behavior. Instead of confessing to God, seeking His forgiveness, and receiving relief from depression,

Cain let his anger keep progressing until it turned into bitterness. In that out-of-control state, he killed Abel. Rather than God's intervention of forgiveness, Cain chose bitterness.

Exasperation is an active and controlling type of anger. This type comes as a result of giving over our mind, will, and emotions to the enemy of our souls: the devil. Usually, transgressors who control others by exasperating them either deny or excuse their own angry behavior. One Old Testament model of active and controlling anger comes from Rachel. "When Rachel saw that she bore Jacob no children, she envied her sister, and said to Jacob, Give me children, or else I will die! And Jacob became very angry with Rachel, and he said, Am I in God's stead, Who has denied you children?" (Gen. 30:1-2 AMP) Since Rachel had neither faced nor worked through her emotional issues, she related through extreme exasperation. That is, she dumped her anger on Jacob instead of going to God to seek His answers, guidance, and provisions for her emotional needs.

Jesus Christ and Others' Sin and Indignation

Christ modeled righteous indignation during two separate occasions when He could no longer hold back a holy reaction to others' sinful pretentiousness. One was the Temple scene described earlier and another was prior to His Olivet Discourse when He retorted to "barbed denunciations" in addressing the Pharisees. They were looked to as "custodians of God's eternal law, authoritative interpreters of the faith, and indefatigable defenders of truth."[6] In interpreting Scripture, they appointed themselves as mediators between the people and God.

Everyday life, in contrast, reveals that they took God's law "and converted it into a basis of self-righteousness."[7] This to them cancelled their need for Christ's death. This behavior represented a continuation of Moses' authority in all generations instead of looking to Jesus for salvation. The Pharisees' unkindness to others by living self-righteous, counterfeit lives brought Christ's strong feelings of indignation against them. That behooves us to beware of any such Pharisaical behavior in our lives.

We can clearly see why Christ did not express bitterness and exasperation. Such angry emotional responses cause us to act out destructive behavior toward others. Jesus Christ did not so relate to anyone at any time. On the other hand, indignation is an emotional response toward any mistreatment being forced onto others. The outrage we may feel over another's mistreatment is closely related to feeling compassion for that one. Compassion, thus, stirs us to do something to help others. When Christ saw His disciples mistreating little children with disrespect and a lack of dignity, He felt a compassionate stirring of "indignation." Jesus showed us how to evaluate a situation that involves disrespect being forced on others.

First, Jesus recognized His disciples' behavior as disrespectful and abusive to children. He did not rationalize or explain away their behavior.

Second, Jesus felt and expressed His angry feelings of indignation toward the disciples. He didn't look the other way or try to excuse or deny His disciples' behavior. He reprimanded them for being unkind and disrespectful to the children.

Third, Jesus acted immediately to change the situation. He commanded them to stop their unjust, abusive behavior immediately and to bring the children to Him so He could bless them with His touch.[8] His example is for us Followers to follow, especially in protecting children. Now is the time for Christians as a Body to respond to killing unborn babies and child abuse with *righteous* **indignation**, as did Christ.

Summarizing Our Thoughts on Jesus Christ and Indignation Over Others' Sin

"So what?" So what that Jesus felt the anger of indignation over others' sin? How can this help you to evaluate a situation which involves disrespect being forced on to others? Like Jesus, you need to recognize your or others' disrespectful and abusive behavior to children or anyone. Like Jesus, you need to "feel" and express angry feelings of indignation toward the guilty person. Don't look the other way or try to excuse or deny behavior that's unkind and disrespectful, especially to the children. Like Jesus did, act immediately to change the situation. Command yourself or others to stop unjust behavior and take children to a safe and reliable source for emotional and spiritual healing. The responsibility is ours to accept the challenge to discover and connect with Jesus Christ's emotions. We're to use His model to help us stay in control when dealing with feelings of indignation over others' sin. In the following chapter, we will discover why Jesus felt the anger of sighing deeply over others' sin.

Chapter Twenty-one

Jesus Felt the Anger of Sighing Deeply Over Others' Sin

And the Pharisees came out
and began to argue with Him,
seeking from Him a sign from heaven, to test Him.
And sighing deeply in His spirit,
[Jesus] said,
"Why does this generation seek for a sign?..."

Mark 8:11-12

"You bunch of snakes! Why do you enjoy arguing with Me? You don't really want to know My answers about heaven; your whole brood is merely testing Me" (Mt. 23:33; Mk. 8:12 par.). Christ and His disciples had just fed 4,000 persons from 7 loaves of bread. In need of rest, they had boated over to the district of Dalmanutha. The Pharisees greeted Him with an argument over whether He would give them a sign from Heaven. When Jesus tried to communicate with them, their arguing sent deep heaving sighs into His insides. After battling with their words, Jesus tired of the foolish empty arguing. He said His heart groaned at the sight of their white-washed doors opening to mental sepulchres, filled with bones deadened from the leprosy of sin. Their hearts were full of sin even though they taught the law and sat in judgment on others. From the heart comes everything we talk about or deal with in life. People who have good stored in the mind naturally bring that "good" out in relating to others. Likewise, those with "evil" stored in the mind bring that out. That is why the Pharisees treated Christ so spitefully; their minds and wills were filled with evil. Their sinful hypocrisy angered Jesus and He told them they were like those who wash the outside of a cup yet leave the inside dirty. As Jesus was leaving them, He said the obstinate bunch would not receive a sign from Him.[1]

Coping With Others' Obstinacy Can Result in Sighing Deeply

The Pharisees of Jesus' day were no different from those of today. They refuse to listen to sound reason, are stubborn, and are unteachable. Obstinacy in others can bring forth from within us an anger of sighing deeply in trying to cope with their sin.[2] Thermometers to gauge degrees of fever are kept in most households. These fever detectors tell us that something within our bodies needs attention. Likewise, anger can act as a detector to tell us something in our lives may be amiss. For instance, our anger may still be frozen in childhood when others' obstinacy hit us with great emotional damage. When we fail to deal with damaged emotions from childhood, we become Pharisaic in refusing sound reason, acting stubborn, and being unteachable.

The Reality of Sighing Deeply

Refusing to deal with damaged emotions can cause problems for us as well as for others. If this continues, we in essence become "obstinacy" for others to deal with, and then create within them the anger of deep sighing. In adulthood if we have not gained skills or courage needed to confront others' obstinacy, the "thought" of confrontation can feel scary. At times we may hear lies from our inner cassette tapes saying words like, "No one helped me when I needed protection; that means I was to blame." Some parents fail to stand in the gap between children and obstinate transgressors of their private margins. Even parents sometimes become obstinate transgressors to their children, causing untold grief and sorrow for them.

Expressing anger through inward groaning and sighing deeply results from many causes. When you feel emotional pain or remember hurtful memories, do you respond with a deep sighing? Most of what we hear about sighing today is usually connected with something romantic. However, Biblical deep sighing comes when some experience angers us to the degree that we draw up sighs from within and inwardly groan. Most of us sigh deeply and groan inwardly quite often when trying to deal with others' sin. Jessy often felt the anger of sighing deeply in trying to deal with an unkind father who could never encourage or accept him. Regardless of how hard he tried to do exactly as his father wanted, the approval never came. As a teenager, Jessy stopped trying to please his father or feel any type of closeness with him. Both stayed their distance and just tolerated each other.

Another Example of Others' Obstinacy

Elizabeth celebrated her third son's eighteenth birthday and three weeks later he was accidently killed. Her son, Fred, was well-liked and a good musician. He was asked to play his guitar one evening with an instrumental group for a benefit in the next town. Two friends went with him. It was early spring and nights were still cool. On returning home, they kept one window rolled down for fresh air since his friend's car wasn't properly ventilated. After dropping off the first friend, Fred decided to roll up the window while driving on home. During those few miles, gas fumes filled the air and their lungs. He had just enough alertness left to stop the car in front of his house before losing consciousness. That's where Elizabeth found them early next morning.

The relationship between Elizabeth and her husband was already strained from his obstinate attitude and abusive behavior to her. Because there was no closeness between them, they could not grieve together over their son's tragic death. She did not have close friends with which to share, and her husband pretended there was nothing to grieve about. His critical attitude toward her for grieving caused a deep depression. When she could not "just snap out of it," he became physically abusive. His cruel, obstinate words and behavior brought up many deep sighs from the bottom of her breast. She groaned inwardly many times before intervention came from a pastor friend.

Jesus Christ and Expressing Anger Through Sighing Deeply

Jesus sighed in connection with serving others and He sighed because of others' sin. Christ sighed and groaned when He prayed for and healed a deaf man with a speech impediment.[3] Evidently Jesus' concern for this man, burdened with limitations, brought up sighs from the bottom of His breast with inward groanings. Later, after He and the disciples fed 4,000 from a few fishes and 7 loaves of bread, they rowed over to Dalmanutha. Immediately the Pharisees came and began to argue with Christ. They were maliciously testing Him by demanding a sign or miracle. In Christ's spirit, He felt the anger of sighing deeply and in agitation asked, "Why do you this generation seek for a sign? I say to you, truly, that no sign shall be given" (Mk. 8:12 par.).

We hear a lot today about codependent behavior, when one does for others what they can and need to do for themselves for their own good. Christ did not choose that route; His time and energy were too valuable to waste on counterfeit seekers. Christ's model of how to cope with others' obstinacy involves three clear choices.

First, Christ *owned* His emotional response. Because Jesus understood that the Pharisees were arguing rather than listening, He groaned and in anger sighed deeply.

Second, Christ *confronted* His verbal attackers. Jesus understood the Pharisees were maliciously testing and not acting out of faith. In anger He challenged them with a question, trying to get them to walk by faith.

Third, Christ *left* them. Because Jesus understood the Pharisees were closed and not open to learning, He did not continue with them. Christ did not try to build a relationship with them, did not try to convince them, and did not take responsibility for their behavior.[4] His practical and workable model is for us to use when we try to cope with others' obstinacy.

Summarizing Our Thoughts on Jesus Christ and Sighing Deeply Over Others' Sin

"So what?" So what that Jesus felt the anger of sighing deeply over others' sin? What does this do for you? Do you have difficulty coping with others' obstinacy? Use Christ's emotional response. Like Jesus, own your emotional response of irritation when you know others are arguing rather than listening. Admit you sometimes feel the anger of inward groaning and sighing deeply. Like Jesus, confront verbal attackers. Challenge them with their malicious testing and refusing to act out of faith. Like Christ, leave them. When others' obstinacy show they are closed and not open to learning, don't stay with them or try to convince them or take responsibility for their behavior. Your time and energy are too valuable to waste on counterfeit seekers. It's up to you to discover and connect with Jesus Christ's emotions; otherwise, His models cannot help you in coping with others' sin. In the next chapter, we will discover why Jesus will feel the anger of fury over others' unrepented sin.

Chapter Twenty-two

Jesus Will Feel the Anger of Fury Over Others' Unrepented Sin

Out of His mouth comes a sharp sword
with which to strike down the nations.
"[Jesus] will rule them with an iron scepter."
He treads the winepress
of the fury of the wrath of God Almighty.
On His robe and on His thigh He has this name written:
King of Kings and Lord of Lords.
Revelation 19:15-16 NIV

"No! Don't worship me. Worship God; He alone is worthy of praise. I am one of God's servants just like you and all your sisters and brothers in Christ" (Rev. 19:10 par.). This mighty angel told me to look at the heavens; very slowly and silently they were opening. A big beautiful white horse of the finest caliber stood obediently under his rider, "The Word of God." Behind Him came the armies of Heaven riding on white horses and dressed in dazzling white linen. "Faithful and True," the rider's second name, has eyes like flashing flames of fire. Many crowns sit on His head; His robe is red with freshly shed blood; His tongue is as powerful as a two-edged sword. With that sword He shall smite nations and rule them with an iron rod one day. Treading with released energy of **fury**, "Faithful and True" will crush all that's not found in His Vineyard. On His robe and thigh I see the title, "King of Kings and Lord of Lords."[1] He's the One we worship.

Controlling Our Fury in Connection With Circumstances

Connecting the King of Kings and Lord of Lords with an unleashed fury is hard for us to visualize. When fury is not controlled, it unleashes intense feelings of hot anger and rage.[2] Most of us are helpless when we innocently get in the way of another's unleashed fury storm. One main reason for unleashed fury in today's society rests on the fact that those "unleashers" have not discovered and connected with Jesus Christ's healthy emotions, for *emotional wholeness*. Yet, one day soon, He will unleash His blast of fury on those who did not repent. Even before leaving this earth the first time, Jesus gave more than adequate and clear Truth about His second coming. As Jesus left, He gave the responsibility of continued forthtelling to us His Followers. We must not get sidetracked from carrying out this "great commission" for the time of His flashing eyes, two-edged sword, and unleashed fury is near.

The Reality of Anyone's Unleashed Fury

Christians as well as non-Christians daily unleash fury onto innocent bystanders. This does not have to be so. We can learn from Christ's model how to control feelings of hot anger and rage, regardless of our emotional pain or circumstances. When we lived in southern California, I had the privilege of spending about eight hours each week for several years at the Los Angeles Mission. I spent a few of those hours each week teaching information regarding counseling tools with the Mission Chaplains. But the major portion of my time was spent counseling the men who had committed their lives to Christ. These men wanted a new life, both emotionally and spiritually. All had come to the Mission from "street life" and suffered from severe emotional losses and pain. Most were trying to withdraw from and stay off illegal drugs. The Chaplains were discipling them in every area of life, preparing them to go back into society as functioning and whole individuals.

Frank's problems in adjusting to the program had proven more complex than most of the other men.[3] Since Frank was a new Christian, he was still learning to spiritually take on the image of Christ. His previous 33 years had been filled with emotional pain and the deprivation of love and acceptance. Those losses built a deep hatred for others into Frank and often he unleashed his fury onto innocent others. His six feet, five inches were filled with rage and great physical strength. These had given him a hell-bent attitude about protecting himself. From the slightest irritation Frank would "flare up" and punch out anyone who happened to be within close range. This had led him into years of crime, as a way of life. When the Chaplains told me that Frank would be coming for counseling, I said, "Thanks a lot, fellows!"

Frank came for counseling because that was an expected part of the program and not because he wanted to participate. At the beginning of his first session, we both felt anxious and wondered about the outcome. I kept remembering the violence that followed him, wondering how he would respond to me. My first question was, "Frank, why have you come for counseling?" I wasn't surprised at his response, "Because the Chaplains see me as an angry person." Even though he was a large, strong, angry man, I felt compassion for him. I wanted to help Frank.

My next question was, "Do you want to know what I see? I see a little boy inside you, deeply hurt." Tears gushed over his cheeks. While others had focused on his anger, I was focusing on the cause of his anger. In order for Frank to survive as a child growing up, he had to protect himself with anger. At a young age, Frank had reached an emotional point where he determined to not let anyone hurt him again. An uncontrolled fury unleashed onto others had become a protective cover-up for his inside pain.

Frank came back again and again to the counseling sessions. As time passed, he began to "see" from Scripture how Christ had handled His anger in dealing with others' obstinacy, emotional hardness, and unkindness. Frank began to learn that some anger, when expressed in a healthy way like Christ did, is okay. The more he learned, the more he understood that anger can be helpful, depending on how we express it and what we are angry about. Frank changed from "inside out." In changing to a more healthy emotional response, he learned to control and to turn from his pent-up fury.

Jesus Christ and Releasing Future Fury

When Christ walked this earth He did not express fury, the intense feeling of hot anger and rage. But soon Christ will come back the second time as King of Kings and Lord of Lords. That's when He will blast those who failed to seek His forgiveness for sin with unleashed hot anger and rage. Woe to those who have rejected His salvation and Lordship offered at Calvary. Ezekiel says an angel will summon all birds that fly across the sky to a "great supper" planned by God. This angel will tell them to "…feast on the flesh of rulers, the flesh of generals and captains, the flesh of powerful and mighty men, the flesh of horses and their riders, and the flesh of all humanity, both free and slave, both small and great!" (Rev. 19:18 AMP) We can see from this Scripture why Christ did not unleash "fury" when He walked on this earth. In refusing to express fury, Jesus showed us how we also can refuse to express that hot anger and rage.

First, Jesus refused to express fury. But He expressed three different types of anger responses in healthy ways and kept them under control.

Second, Jesus understood and appreciated the destructive nature of fury. He knew we needed His model to help us learn to control our fury.

Third, Jesus has reserved His fury for the future. One day He will unleash it on those not found in His Vineyard—whose sins are unforgiven.[4] Christ's anger models show us that "many people don't get angry when they should and therefore do not mobilize the energy necessary to deal with some crucially important issues of life."[5] Jesus' healthy anger responses show us how to express as well as how to control our feelings of anger.

Summarizing Our Thoughts on Jesus Christ and Feeling Fury Over Unrepented Sin

"So what?" So what that Jesus Christ will someday feel the anger of fury over others' unrepented sin? What can that do for you today in trying to deal with your or others' unleashed fury? Like Jesus, refuse to express the destructive and hot anger of fury. Under the Holy Spirit's guidance, learn to express the same types of anger that Christ did and for the same type of reasons. Like Jesus, understand and appreciate the destructive nature of fury. Don't allow the devil to goad you into expressing that hot anger during trying circumstances. Like Jesus, reserve your feelings of fury for the future to use against satan, the enemy of your soul. It's your responsibility to discover and connect with Jesus Christ's healthy model of reserving fury for the future. If you don't, He cannot help you contain your feelings of hot anger in healthy ways. In the next chapter, we will discover why Jesus felt amazed in dealing with life's dilemmas.

Chapter Twenty-three

Jesus Felt Amazed
in
Dealing With Life's Dilemmas

....Sit down here while I pray.
And [Jesus] took with Him Peter and James and John,
and began to be struck with
terror and amazement....

Mark 14:32-33 AMP

"Wake up men! I hear bootsteps, you can sleep later; here comes My betrayer!" (Mk. 14:42 par.) The "little band of 12" had learned from and lived with Jesus for three years as He poured His very Life into them. Earlier that day, they had spent several hours as the guests of Simon the leper. He had prepared, served, and shared with them a special passover supper. In the midst of that unique time a stressful dilemma developed when Jesus confronted Peter. "Before the rooster's morning wake-up call you will deny Me not only once, but three times." Although the night was warm, cold chills ran through Peter as he heard those words. Even while Peter insisted emphatically that he would never desert Christ, a clammy and sickening shame oozed over the depth of his inner being. Christ was aware of his shame, but He knew that dilemmas would continue until Peter learned to control impulsive behavior. Later, Jesus would stoop down to pick up and replace a soldier's bloody ear, whacked off by Peter's impulsiveness. Christ and His band of 11 walked toward Gethsemane. Entering the Garden, Jesus felt terror and building alarm as He was facing His dilemma of the cross.[1]

Feeling Amazed in Dealing With Dilemmas

Within a few hours the devil's followers, with evil and "dark angels" cheering them on, would crucify Christ by nailing spikes into His flesh.

Thinking about the approaching physical, emotional, mental, and spiritual pain sent shivers of terror and great alarm through Christ's emotional system. Later, while praying earnestly about submitting to the cross, He again felt those feelings of amazement.[2] These feelings caused a heavy perspiration to ooze from each pore and soak His clothing. Although Christ had described His betrayal and subsequent death on a cross to the disciples, they could not grasp the horror and reality of those words.

On the whole, neither do we. Therefore, most of us cannot recognize or relate to the "feelings of terror and great alarm" that Christ felt as He labored in a prayer battle. Christ's teaching in Matthew 6 and 7 reveal that prayer consists of both the human and the Divine. The human part is asking and receiving while the Divine part is giving.[3] Involved with the human part is a dimension called enemy-opposition that's inspired by the devil to oppose us. One type of opposition is His often whispered lies. "God does not answer your prayers for He doesn't understand your dilemmas. I'm your answer; you can't get along without me. Worship me and I'll give you the world." We need to remember that Jesus would not listen to the devil's lies. Instead, He agonized in warfare prayer until the capillaries ruptured and sweat dribbled down His forehead like drops of blood. Warfare praying calls for a commitment of time and energy few of us are willing to give, even when dealing with dilemmas.

The Reality of Dilemmas and Needed Prayer

Even though each of us sometimes faces dilemma, none can equal that of Christ facing death on the cross. Like in Christ's life, some of our dilemmas call for warfare praying. A lazy request like "Bless us, our friends, and the world, amen" is not battling in prayer during a dilemma. Warfare praying is new for a large portion of Christians; but it is not new. Failure to recognize the warfare aspects of prayer keeps many Christians from developing an effective prayer life. That failure also testifies to satan's successful strategy for keeping the Body of Christ as a whole from understanding just how critical is the need for warfare prayer. As a result of an ineffective prayer life, discouragement takes over. We must understand that warfare "prayer is striking the winning blow at the concealed enemy."[4] This needs to be true of all prayer life, not only with dilemma.

Often we think of a dilemma as a problem that we are incapable of satisfactorily resolving on our own. We seek information from others and wisdom from God through Scripture and prayer. Seeking His wisdom in prayer can become a battle since satan—the enemy of our souls—interrupts, interferes with, and opposes us on every hand. Yet, some dilemmas develop quickly and unexpectedly, interfering with time for prolonged prayer. Such circumstances call for prayer as we go. Earthquakes don't give warning. Suddenly the house begins to shake. A loud noise like a roaring freight train fills the air; dishes begin to rattle; chandeliers swing back and forth; pictures fall off the wall; bookcases and china cabinets overturn; and some houses slide off their foundation. During our first earthquake, the few seconds it lasted seemed like hours. All six of us shook with feelings of terror and great alarm. We did indeed pray in the midst of a dilemma that was beyond our ability to solve.

Praying obeys Christ's command, strengthens us to move ahead, and helps us deal with life's dilemmas during times of amazement. There are times when God's answers are different from what we had hoped or asked; sometimes the answer is "no." The God-man knows about receiving "No" during a most intense warfare prayer time. That, however, did not alter His faith and trust in the Almighty Father. We also must believe that His ways and thoughts of the overall picture are above our understanding. He does not leave us in doubt about His will, although the enemy opposition tries to deceive us into doubting the Lord. God's directions are for our good. With our cooperation, He will ultimately in time bring for us the best solution.

Feelings of Terror and Alarm in Childhood

When Christ was trying to deal with whether or not to submit to His Father's will, He suffered from terror and alarm. Jesus knew He needed help in His long, drawn-out struggle and spent hours in concentrated prayer. But when situations develop quickly, we don't always have time for concentrated prayer. To others looking in, it might look like we're trying to handle situations in our strength or knowledge rather than calling on God's wisdom. But that's not true for those who have learned through prayer to "strike the winning blow at the concealed enemy" as they move quickly.

Norma experienced several unexpected and traumatic dilemmas in her early teens. She remembers feeling the most terror and great alarm during the first one. Since her parents didn't know how to deal with problems caused by the heaviness of life, their relationship was very strained. Their loud arguing awakened her early one morning, sending a feeling of alarm through her young body. Instantly, because of emotional devastation from previous arguments, the nerves in her stomach curled into small tight knots causing a queasy feeling. By the time Norma ran to the dining room dilemma, her father's angry shouts had become hard slaps and shoves on her mother's face and body. As Norma's mother was falling, she saw an amazement on her face. Realizing her physical power did not equal this trauma, feeling terror Norma quickly ran for help and prayed as she ran. God immediately answered Norma's prayer for help. Years later she understood with Nehemiah that at times it's short prayers combined with quick action that are God's solution in time of unexpected trauma (see Neh. 1–2).

In dealing with the aftermath of a dilemma it's helpful to pray Scripture, like Colossians 3:12. Father help me "put on a heart of compassion, kindness, humility, gentleness and patience; bearing with [others] and forgiving [others]; just as [You] Lord forgave me" (paraphrased). We need long, concentrated times of faith-filled prayer to prepare us for the quick times of action. This will help us learn how to listen to the Holy Spirit's voice and submit our will to God's design. Regardless of cost, the emotional security gained from prayer helps motivate us to face and deal with dilemma.

Feelings of Terror and Alarm in Adulthood

New York City residents know about all kinds of terror and alarm. Some years ago while single and working on the New York Billy Graham Crusade office staff, I lived in a Manhattan Seminary men's residence. Electric eyes for door security had not yet been installed and an older man worked as a doorguard. One evening walking home from the office, a young man approached me to talk. He asked to enter the building with me but I told him "No, you can't go in." He then threatened to do harm to me and the older doorguard. Even though I felt a good deal of alarm at his words, I knew he could not be allowed to enter our building.

When I opened the outside door to enter, he tried to push through with me. That started a scrabble. The intruder slammed his fist through the glass door striking our doorkeeper's face, breaking his glasses, and bloodying his nose. At that point I grabbed the intruder, punched him, and pushed him outside. With blood dripping from his cut hand, he started running up the sidewalk with me after him. About that time police arrived so I left them with the chase while I went back to help our doorkeeper.

The male intruder had wanted in our building so he could try to sexually connect with other males. Since such behavior goes against God's moral standards, He intervened quickly on our behalf. There was prayer in my mind while my body was giving protection during a trauma of amazement and great alarm. Whether a prayer is short or long, petitioning God to help those being attacked or being held captive by the devil's schemes is the hard work of warfare praying.[5]

Like with all soldiers well-prepared for battle, we Christian Soldiers must prepare also for battle. We can expect to be shot at when going into spiritual war against the enemy of our souls. That's why it is important to incorporate Christ's teaching in Luke 18:1 where we're told to always pray and not give up. After gathering together Christ's words on prayer, one can see that His answers give the proof of whether we and our prayers are acceptable to the Heavenly Father. Christ didn't tell us to consider His gifts of higher value than fellowship or favour of the Father. By no means. Jesus wants prayer answers to represent a token of His favour plus the reality of our fellowship with Him.[6] While dilemma and prayer go together like hand in glove, prayer time must not be put off or limited to trying times. Fellowship with our Savior and Lord Jesus Christ must hold a prominent place in our schedules whether we walk in peaceful or trying times.

Jesus Christ and Dilemmas and Amazement

When Christ walked on earth, He had to cope with many different types of dilemmas and emotional responses. One instance was His disciples' disappointing behavior of failing to stand in the "prayer gap" with Him. Before entering warfare prayer, Christ shared His deepest emotional needs. "Men, My soul is exceedingly sorrowful unto emotional death" (Mk. 14:34 par.). Under heavy burden, Christ asked the disciples to participate in prayer for and with Him. He then walked away a short distance and started seriously talking with God. Later, He came back to the disciples for their input and encouragement. Despite Christ's earlier transparency, they hadn't gotten any further than their tiredness. They seemed unaware of His need for their support.

Christ directly confronted Peter, "Simon, are you asleep? Could you not keep watch for one hour?" (Mk. 14:37) Then He told the three, "Keep awake *and* watch and pray (constantly) that you may not enter into temptation; the spirit indeed is willing, but the flesh is weak" (Mk. 14:38

AMP). Christ returned to another serious talk with His Holy Father. A second time, He came back and found the men still in a sleepy mental daze. They could not grasp Christ's urgent request for them to "pray" and "feel" with Him. Despite this deep disappointment, He returned to His private place to again agonize in prayer over death on a cross. This time, Christ reached the place of submitting His human will to God's Divine will. In this peaceful state, Jesus came a third time to His sleeping disciples. "Okay men, enough sleeping and resting. It's time to get up and go; My betrayer is at hand" (Mk. 14:41-42 par.).

In dealing with His disciples, Christ demonstrated how to let others reap what they sow. This New Testament principle located in Galatians 6:7 discourages codependent relationships. Rather, Christ's healthy model shows us how to continue with God-given responsibilities when the devil tries to distract and discourage us through a dilemma designed by others.

First, Christ chose to be vulnerable with His innermost feelings. He did not deny or rationalize His emotional struggle with His most difficult situation.

Second, Christ confronted the situation through concentrated prayer. He fought the spiritual battle of warfare prayer with God, which prepared Him for either quick or prolonged action.

Third, Christ submitted His human will to God's Divine will. His submission to God strengthened Him for the immediate as well as for the next season of battle.[7]

With the number of angry and out-of-control people on the rise, it is encouraging to know that Christ's healthy, workable process for times of amazement is still relevant today.

Summarizing Our Thoughts on Jesus and Dilemmas and Feeling Amazed

"So what?" So what that Jesus felt amazed in dealing with life's dilemmas? What does this do for you? Are you struggling with a dilemma that's causing you to feel terror and great alarm? Don't do as the disciples when they failed to accept their reality. Use Christ's model of being vulnerable with His feelings. Talk with a trusted friend or Christian counselor about the situation. Like Christ, do not deny or rationalize your emotional struggle; confront the situation through concentrated prayer with God. Ask praying friends to do battle with you using warfare prayer. Like Christ, submit your human will to God's Divine will. Through the Holy

Spirit, continue with God-given responsibilities when satan through others or through situations tries to distract or discourage you. In the next chapter we will discover why Jesus marveled in dealing with life's dilemmas.

Chapter Twenty-four

Jesus Marveled
in
Dealing With Life's Dilemmas

And He was not able to do even one work
of power there, except
that He laid His hands on a few
sickly people [and] cured them.
And He marveled because of their unbelief—
their lack of faith in Him....

Mark 6:5-6 AMP

"Lord, my servant is lying paralyzed at home, suffering intense pain; but I'm not fit or worthy for You to come under my roof. But if You will just say the word, I know my beloved servant will be healed" (Mt. 8:5-9 par.). The military officer's faithful servant had not felt well for quite some time, but the doctor could not make an exact diagnosis. After a weakening paralysis moved over the servant's legs, they knew he suffered from palsy. As a friend and as a servant, he was important to the centurion. In great grief and concern the military officer began an intense search for a cure. After hearing of a man called Christ and His power to heal, the centurion went immediately in search of Him. At that particular time is when He entered Capernaum. When the officer saw Jesus, he went to Him for help. After the centurion expressed the belief that Christ could heal even without His seeing the servant, feelings of astonishment and surprise went over Jesus. In a state of marvel He exclaimed to those who had gathered that in all Israel He had not found such great faith with anyone.[1]

Marveling in the Face of Others' Responses

Responding to circumstances in surprise or astonishment during Christ's time and calling the response "marvel" was evidently uncommon.[2] It remains so even in today's society for emotional expression. Yet, this emotion is recorded twice of Christ. On one day He marveled at the Capernaum centurion's great faith in regards to his servant's healing. On another day, Christ marveled at people in the synagogue from His own country because of their failure to believe. It is interesting to note that Christ was struck with surprise and astonishment both at people's response of unbelief as well as their response of faith.

This contrast seems to bear out the view that society, culture, and personal experiences help to determine what triggers our emotional responses.[3] We see this same idea presented by the beloved apostle. Christ decided to return to Galilee, by way of Samaria. Feeling tired, He sat down at Jacob's well while the disciples went to buy food. When a Samaritan woman came to draw water, Jesus asked her for a drink. In surprise she asked, "Why are you, a Jew, asking me, a female Samaritan, for a drink? You know the Jews have nothing to do with Samaritans" (Jn. 4:9 par.). Choosing His words carefully, Christ talked to the woman in such a way that helped her feel accepted and valued. His kind response triggered in her a response of astonishment. A feeling of marvel prompted the woman to leave her water pot and find others to tell about Christ's bold kindness. She also explained to them about the Living Water for Samaritans (see Jn. 4:4-30).

The Reality of Marveling at Others' Responses

His disciples arrived about that time with food. Upon seeing and hearing Christ talking with a Samaritan woman, they marveled. Although the disciples responded in surprise and astonishment, they squelched a desire to ask Christ why He crossed over cultural communication lines. Their walk with Jesus had not, evidently, cleared their thinking in regards to self-esteem and personal worth. It's apparent the disciples had not learned that "how" we see others is the way we "treat" them. When we "see" others as worthless, we will treat them as worthless. But when we "see" others as persons of worth to Christ, we will communicate worth to them in the way we talk to and treat them. Most Believers today believe that Jesus Christ died for, accepts, and forgives "all" regardless of cultural communication lines. Yet, while these Believers have settled the salvation question, many have not settled the personal-worth issue.

Many of these same Believers are struck with surprise and astonishment at the thought that Jesus, Son of God, provides the basis of self-esteem and personal worth for "all" regardless of cultural communication differences. His creative acts of creation and salvation correspond to help us feel both loved by God and a belonging to God. We cannot work for salvation. According to Ephesians 2:8-9, it's God's free gift. Likewise, our personal worth is a free gift from God; we cannot work for it. That's why different skin colors, different financial levels, or different social levels matter not to Christ. He is skin-color blind with no financial or social preferences. His responses to others are in regard to their heart problems or conditions felt in opposition to God. He gives His worth and Living Water to all who believe in Him.

Since Christ knew who He was, the only begotten Son of God, His self-identity and personal worth were well established. Self-acceptance enabled Him to interact with and respond to everyone through love and acceptance. Many of us have not reached that well-established stage. "There's an important truism about self-identity. Our self-picture determines the way we feel about ourselves and others...[for those] who feel self-acceptance picture themselves with a strong self-concept. They feel more healthy emotions than [those] who struggle with a weak self-concept."[4]

Many of us have not recognized that from God's view, we are persons of worth. For this reason we don't need to marvel at such words as self-image or personal worth. An old Chinese proverb says, "It's easier to believe a *lie* you've heard a thousand times than to believe a *truth* you've heard for the first time." The Old Testament gives us this truth, "God said, Let Us [Father, Son, and Holy Spirit] make mankind in Our image, after Our likeness.... So God created man in His own image, in the image *and* likeness of God He created him; male and female He created them" (Gen. 1:26-27 AMP). Being created in God's image means that we are persons of worth. This is the basis for our self-identity. That is why we no longer need to strive for self-identity through the "good works" of comparing, performing, and competing. Accepting that truth can motivate us to begin discovering and connecting with Christ's emotions, which is the only prescription for emotional wholeness. What a marvel.

One Example of Marveling Over Another's Response

Each of us has the need for "belongingness" and being loved, for they influence our *feelings* about who we are. We've agreed that being created in God's image with mind, soul, and emotions provides the basis for self-image and personal worth. Understanding this can affect our attitude toward using spiritual gifts. "God has not equally distributed gifts, talents, or intelligence, but He has equally distributed Himself. Our sense of worth [then] comes from knowing who we are as children of God,"[5] created in His image. That's why the basis of personal worth rests on God's worth. Since His worth is immeasurable, our worth is also immeasurable. Yet, having God's worth and "being worthy of His love" are not the same. We can do absolutely nothing, zero, to be worthy. We cannot work for personal worth; it is God's free gift.

Harold learned this the hard way. He had finished four grueling years of medical school and accepted an assignment for his residency. He not only worked long hours to learn medical information, he had also worked for feelings of false self-esteem. During the long schooling time, his mind, soul, and emotions were depleted leaving him weak and vulnerable to the enemy's attacks. In this depleted emotional state, he met a woman doctor at his resident hospital who was overly responsive to him. Harold forgot his commitments of holiness to God, faithfulness to his wife, and wholeness to himself. As he lived this double, emotionally painful, and unfruitful life, his wife lived in a state of surprise and astonishment at Harold's changed life. After many long months, she finally packed his clothes, set them on the porch, and told him to go.

God used this to shake Harold into reality and he chose recommitment. Once he made a recommitment to God, wife, and self, his life daily took on new meaning and wholeness. Harold learned that "status" cannot give personal worth. He discovered that the only real and healthy feelings of self-esteem are based on God's worth. This truth took away his works of comparing, performing, and competing. He understood that "To be in the image of God means to be in a complementary (not competitive) relationship to him, to be in correspondence."[6] Harold now lives in a complementary relationship with God, his wife, and his children. Christ's blessings on his new life cause him to marvel in appreciation.

Jesus Christ and Dealing With Dilemmas and Responding With Marvel

With all emotional responses to dilemma, there's always a set of circumstances. In counseling with people I've found one of the most common problems is their inability to deal with life's dilemmas. When one is in crisis and cannot see any hope, the primary motivator enabling us to face dilemmas, the tendency is to give up. Yet, in facing the hardest circumstance, Christ did not give up. He knew that death was not the end for Him. This was evidenced when He cried out on the cross, "It is finished! ... Father, into Your hands I commit My spirit!" (Jn. 19:30; Lk. 23:46b AMP)

Christ made that final choice because He clung to hope. Doing this, He showed us how to cling to hope.

Many of us in facing a life dilemma forget hope and run. Christ neither ran nor tried to pretend that dying on a cross would be easy. "Father, My hour is come. Now glorify Thy Son, that I may be able to glorify Thee. You gave Me authority over all mankind so that to all whom Thou has given Me, I may give eternal life" (Jn. 17:1-2 par.). Accepting the Father's death assignment, filled with indescribable pain, made the God-man even more strong in His modeling how to deal with life dilemmas.

In dealing with reality that His time on the cross had come, Christ sought a broader perspective for His mind's picture. He saw in a new way that "the cross" was part of His Father's will. "My food is to do the will of Him who sent Me, and to accomplish His work. ... I can do nothing on My own initiative. As I hear, I judge; and My judgment is just, because I do not seek My own will, but the will of Him who sent Me" (Jn. 4:34; 5:30). Our Lord had dealt with His particular dilemma. The God-man, living in a fully human body like yours and mine, gave us a clear and workable model to use during times of marveling over others' responses.

First, Christ faced or acknowledged His reality. He did not try to reduce, change, dilute, or deny a troublesome circumstance. Submission to God's Divine will brought Him inner peace.

Second, Christ looked for and got a broad perspective on the problem. He didn't dwell on physical death or despair; He communicated with God, His reliable source. Submission to God's Divine will brought Him emotional stability.

Third, Christ clung to hope. He did not give up or cave in to hopelessness and despair.[7] Submission to God's Divine will brought Christ the hope that after death He would return to His Father. That hope helped Him endure the cross, even though He despised the shame, and then sit down at the right hand of God's throne.

Summarizing Our Thoughts on Jesus and Dilemma and Marveling

"So what?" So what Jesus marveled in dealing with others' responses during life dilemmas? How can that help you deal with your dilemmas? Like Christ did, you can face and acknowledge your reality. In doing that, you won't need to reduce or change or deny a troublesome circumstance. Like Christ, you can look for a broad perspective on the problem. In so doing, look for a reliable source that can help you avoid dwelling on physical, emotional, or spiritual despair. Like Christ, cling to hope. Don't give up or cave in to despair or hopelessness. Jesus Christ is always our answer when dealing with others' responses. In the following chapter we will discover why Christ felt deeply moved during times of loss.

Chapter Twenty-five

Jesus Felt Deeply Moved During Times of Loss

When Jesus therefore saw [Mary] weeping,
and the Jews who came with her,
also weeping,
He was deeply moved in spirit....

John 11:33

"Jesus healed one from blindness but He couldn't heal His dear friend Lazarus" (Jn. 11:37 par.). Mary and Martha misunderstood Jesus' motive for waiting two days before coming to be with them. They agreed with their Jewish friends that He could not really help them. Often people saw Him as no different from them, failing to see His excellence of character in each healthy emotional response. After Jesus healed the centurion officer's servant in Capernaum, He traveled down to Nain a town about five miles south and east of Nazareth. As Christ and His disciples entered the city gate, they met a funeral procession. A widowed mother and friends walked behind a casket, which carried her only son. Earlier, Jesus had tried through Lazarus' death to show His followers the difference between God's power over death and the formal Pharisaic belief in the resurrection.[1] So without talking to the widowed mother, this time He just touched the casket and told the man to "Arise!" He sat up and started talking. Through this "raising" Jesus was trying to teach them the deep movement of compassion rather than resurrection. Seeing the widowed mother grieving over the loss of her only son caused Jesus to remember Mary and Martha's grief over Lazarus' death and His own deep movement of anger as He groaned in the spirit. Actually, those around Him had heard the groan as a snort of anger. His anger was not as much toward the sisters' disbelief for Lazarus' immediate return to life as it was toward humanity's devastating enemy of death.[2]

Feeling Deeply Moved in Times of Loss

Times of loss come in multi-shades of color or experience, not just in connection with death. Women are usually known for being emotionally stronger than men. Depending on their individual personality and background, they usually deal more realistically with loss. Sadly, our society still lives with the myth that men or boys should not show vulnerability in painful emotional situations. Because of this wrongly taught myth, most of them learn to suppress and deny their "real" emotions having to do with loss. Over a period of time, such suppression builds and stores anger. With the slightest provocation, this unhealthy anger spills over onto innocent bystanders. When Jesus walked the earth, He modeled anger in healthy ways trying to discourage anger suppression and denial. He knows such behaviors can lead to anger progression, which produces only damaging and destructive behavior. Scripture shows us clearly that Christ was open, direct, and forthright in expressing His emotions. Consequently, Jesus neither suppressed nor denied His emotional responses. He was deeply moved toward His close friends' emotional needs in time of loss with a "physical shudder" as a snort of anger.[3]

The Reality of Loss

What's the greatest loss you've had to deal with? In childhood, my greatest loss was not experiencing "closeness" with my parents and the resulting devastation in my emotional life. Jane's greatest loss in childhood was her parents' destructive relationship and the resulting devastation in her emotional life. In adulthood, our greatest loss began in the fall of 1990 when, one by one, our four adult children's repressed memories of satanic ritual abuse started surfacing. When we think about the evil and devastating crimes forced on our children, we feel deeply moved with anger for them in their loss, like Christ felt with His close friends in their loss.

In examining Jesus' different responses of anger, in each case we see that His responses are the anger of love. Such is true of all righteous anger, which is an anger directed toward evil. This is why we can say that anger is often mixed with love. Anger is the emotion produced by hostility, and by its very nature love is hostile to everything that causes injury to life.[4] Injury to life always brings us loss. Our children's severe losses were their innocence, security, safety, and ability to trust. We should have represented trust, safety, and security to provide them with a sweet, innocent childhood. But the evil satanic crimes cost them their safety, security, everything innocent to children, and the ability to trust. These great losses caused them to feel deeply moved.

Coping With Childhood Loss

Shortly after Donald's[5] 29th birthday, God through the Holy Spirit's power started him in a process of memory retrieval. Little by little, as he could endure the emotional shock, God opened his memories. Beginning when he was three, over a three-year span, next-door neighbors secretly took him and a sister to various types of occultic meetings. They were forced to watch satanic rituals where little children were tortured and killed. In God's mercy, memories surface sparingly since He knows they leave survivors devastated emotionally, physically, spiritually, and mentally. For their healing to come, precious survivors must receive nurturing care, acceptance, and love from a Christ-designed Community (talked about in Chapter Nine). The entire Christian community must come to terms with the truth that healing for emotional, mental, or spiritual loss takes **time**, just as does physical healing. To help and encourage those hurting emotionally, we must learn to follow Christ's example of feeling deeply moved with others during their times of loss.

Coping With Adulthood Loss

Chuck Colson is known to thousands for his years of service as special counsel to President Nixon during the early 1970's. But some don't know that after Watergate, while serving a prison sentence, he was "born again." Now, as a Christian, Chuck is known nationally for his challenging, credible books and Prison Fellowship Ministries. He has spoken numerous times about his loss of freedom and how that affected his life. One time Chuck described how it felt to return to Alabama's Maxwell Federal Prison where he served his prison term. Entering Maxwell to speak to the 250 inmates, memories of *time* spent there almost overwhelmed him. Chuck remembered being told when to eat, where to walk, and when he could visit with his wife. "Feelings of helplessness, frustration, a sense that the walls were closing in" reminded him afresh of his personal loss of freedom.

One night while observing those inmates' looks of hope and expectation as they awaited his message, he felt encouraged. Chuck explained, "I was deeply moved as I realized how, when I least expected it, God had used my failure, my imprisonment, to spark a movement of His people, reaching 600 prisons across the country."[6] Since that statement, hundreds more of prisons even in other countries have been reached by Chuck Colson and the Prison Fellowship Ministries. Mr. Colson learned from Christ's model to feel deeply moved during times of loss, not just for his but also for others'.

Jesus Christ and Loss and Feeling Deeply Moved

Lazarus' door was always open to Jesus, even when many others were slammed shut. When Jesus was misunderstood by others, fellowship and acceptance always awaited Him at the Lazarus home. The deep friendship shared equally between them with Mary and Martha, was special to Jesus. He appreciated their uniqueness. Of the three, Martha was aggressive in action, possessive, and verbal. Mary was assertive in action, studious, and emotional. Lazarus, with parents gone, was head of their home. He was faithful in overseeing the family possessions and was a loving brother, evidenced by Mary and Martha's devotion to him.[7]

Jesus did not try to rush them into healing and restoration, but nurtured them by meeting their unique and personal needs. He was their link between life and death. During Mary and Martha's time of loss, He felt deeply moved by their emotional pain. Yet, Christ's snort of anger went deeper than the compassion felt for their loss. Earlier, before the "Jews" had come with Mary to the Teacher, they had sought to stone Him. In addition, they had resolved to cut off from all religious and social intercourse everyone who acknowledged Jesus as the Messiah. Now, Jesus sees them trailing along with Mary in pretense of being her friend. "With hearts full of hatred they can profess to be comforters, and can mingle their tears with hers. It is this hypocrisy which now stirs in His spirit an anger so intense that it causes nerve and muscle and limb to tremble beneath its force."[8] Trying to deal with their hypocrisy while at the same time cope with great loss, caused within Jesus a deep movement of anger. He showed us how to avoid denying "true" feelings during times of loss.

First, Jesus observed and evaluated the situation. He looked behind their crying and tears in order to see the true needs being presented.

Second, Jesus responded with sincere vulnerability. Even in front of others, the God-man expressed a strong agitation of mind and emotion without shame.

Third, Jesus overruled masking and pretense in time of loss by His genuineness. He demonstrated the importance of responding to others with sincerity during times of loss.[9] His practical model is for each of us to connect with.

Summarizing Our Thoughts on Jesus and Loss and Feeling Deeply Moved

"So what?" So what that Jesus felt deeply moved during times of loss? What does that do for you? Do you sometimes struggle with "true" feelings during your own times of loss? Do you sometimes struggle with trying to be genuine when others are suffering loss? Try using Jesus Christ's emotional responses. Like Christ, you can observe and evaluate the situation. You can look behind crying and tears in order to see true needs being presented. Like Christ, you can respond with sincere openness. Even in front of others, you can express your agitation of mind and emotion without shame. As did Christ, let your genuineness overrule any tendency to mask or pretend in time of loss. You can demonstrate the importance of responding to others during times of loss with sincerity, rather than pretense. It's your responsibility to discover and connect with the emotional responses of Jesus; otherwise, His models cannot help you in times of loss. In the next chapter, we will discover why Jesus felt sad during times of loss.

Chapter Twenty-six

Jesus Felt Sad
During
Times of Loss

Then Jesus went with [the disciples]
to a place called Gethsemane....
Then He said to them,
My soul is very sad....

Matthew 26:36,38 AMP

"My soul is very sad...so that I am almost dying" (Mt. 26:38 AMP). Celebrating His last passover supper with the disciples, Jesus blessed bread, broke it, and told them to eat. Then He prayed over the cup and told them to drink. To end the special celebration, they sang a worshipful hymn, thanked their kind host, and left. Christ often walked in the gardens surrounding Jerusalem. About three-fourths of a mile east of Jerusalem is where busy workers could be seen crushing oil from olives in the Garden of Gethsemane. That Garden was a frequent resort for Jesus and His disciples. Its beauty and peacefulness helped them relax and rest, away from large crowds, during the "tempestuous Jerusalem ministry." This particular night seemed different from the many other times they had spent in the Garden. Instead of His usual cheerfulness, Jesus seemed sad and weary like one in a deep grieving mode. When they entered Gethsemane, Peter and the Zebedee brothers walked with Jesus into the Garden's deep shadow. Jesus shared with them how sad and depressed He felt. Then He asked them to stand in the prayer gap with Him. Jesus needed their emotional and prayerful support as He dealt with an inner turmoil of sadness during loss.[1]

Sadness That's Okay in Time of Loss

When we look at Jesus only as Deity, it's difficult to "see" that He experienced *loss* as the God-man. We must never minimize Jesus' loss through the indescribable physical pain that He suffered. Yet in a different way, the burden of your and my sin pressing heavily on Him caused an even greater loss. A spiritual loss came when He was "made sin for us"; this separated Him emotionally from His Heavenly Father.[2] Anticipating that loss is why Christ's soul was very sad, almost to the point of death. We feel sad in situations and circumstances that encompass us with grief.[3] Jesus felt loss when His disciples failed to stand with Him in prayer. He grieved when Jerusalem would not turn to Him for salvation. Christ's healthy and balanced model shows there is sadness that's okay in time of loss. In fact, when we don't feel sad in the face of grief we're denying and cutting off our normal, healthy God-given emotions. According to Jesus, it's okay to feel sad during loss.

The Reality of Unhealthy Sadness

Life provides countless experiences that cause loss and give reason for sadness. Yet, numerous groups of Christians who have not discovered or connected with Jesus' healthy, whole, and balanced emotional responses still try to deny their sad feelings. Their unfounded belief says Christians should always carry around light smiles, regardless of their heavy hearts. They either have forgotten or are not aware of King David's advice against denying or suppressing our emotions in Psalm 32:3,6. David said that when he kept silent instead of expressing his sadness his bones wasted away. That's another way of saying he became depressed. He also said that silence, or unhealthy sadness, kept him from going to God when the waters of trial overflowed him. David allowed outward circumstances to loom larger than God and very quickly his emotions overcame him.[4] Yes, Christians who deny their sad feelings will benefit greatly from studying Jesus' unpharisaical and genuine emotional responses.

Once a rich young ruler came to Jesus seeking eternal life. Jesus talked to him about keeping the commandments. His response was that he had kept them from his youth. Then Jesus told him to sell all that he possessed and give the cash to those who were in need. When the young man heard that, he felt very sad. Yet, Jesus didn't condemn him for his sadness. Christ's concern was over the man's self-centered heart condition that kept him from sharing with others. The God-man wanted this young man to understand that happiness does not consist of "things" or "money." Jesus told him that a camel walking through the eye of a needle is an easier feat than one person trying to enter God's kingdom by using his riches. He was trying to teach that young ruler the difference between developing a relationship with Him and basing security on material wealth. His inability to make that emotional switch left him with an unhealthy sadness.

One Example of Healthy Sadness

Shortly before receiving her BS degree in elementary education, Sally received her "Mrs." degree. She eagerly entered the field of teaching while Gil entered seminary in preparation to teach on the college level. Sally enjoyed teaching children, but from childhood she had looked forward to having her own. Their busy and frantic schedules caused much stress for them, but Sally knew she had to persevere during her Gil's years of schooling. After about four years, a physical, mental, and emotional cycle developed. She eagerly waited each month for evidence that a conception had occurred; but each month her menses would appear. During her menses, she often felt sick. This monthly physical change told Sally that her hoped-for pregnancy had not happened. Month after month this unwanted situation would encompass Sally with grief and replace her hope with a very sad feeling.

After much prayer and talk, Sally and Gil decided to try to adopt children. Strict regulations and long waiting lists discouraged them. But believing God was in charge, they persevered. They were amazed and thrilled at God's ways of intervening, enabling them to adopt. Much sooner than they thought, a precious baby girl was assigned to them for adoption. On the way home, Sally asked her husband to stop the car. She unwrapped her precious baby to count fingers and toes. Yes, she had a beautiful, perfect baby. Looking at that special baby caused Sally to panic. She thought, "Lord, I'm not capable of raising this child; I don't deserve such a perfect baby." Day by day those feelings began to shrink and Sally started to feel confidence and assurance that God would enable her to finish the awesome task. Before adoption could be completed, they had to wait six months to see if the biological mother would change her mind. As the waiting period ended, a precious baby boy was also assigned to them. God had lovingly and generously filled their quiver full.

As Sally sees women who are not able to conceive, she feels a sadness for them. When she learns of young women who conceived babies outside of marriage, she feels an extreme sadness. She longs to be able to share with them the importance of living by God's standards for personal purity and choosing to conceive only in the emotional bond of marriage. Almost 40 years later, Sally still feels grateful to God for blessing her with two beautiful babies to raise for His glory. Because Sally was willing to live by God's design He blessed her with children, the desire of her heart. Some continue to live with unhealthy sadness because they will not choose God's design. Sally has learned that when we cooperate with God's time and way, He can and will rule over loss to help us deal with our sadness.

Jesus Christ and Loss and Sadness

Jesus experienced loss at different times in His life on earth. As Jesus lived with the consequences of others' sin, He was confronted with an abundance of sad situations. When King Herod learned of Jesus' birth, he believed the devil's lies that Christ intended to replace him as a king. He became consumed with evil jealousy. Wanting to protect his throne, Herod tried to find Jesus so he could kill Him. To protect Jesus, Mary and Joseph had to leave their homeland to go into hiding. This caused Jesus to suffer loss of physical security. Later, at age 30, He started His ministry and suffered financial loss; He did not even own a pillow for His head at night. He once told His followers that, "[God] makes His sun rise on the wicked and on the good, and makes the rain fall upon the upright and the wrongdoers [alike]" (Mt. 5:45 AMP). The God-man did not consider His losses as such; He accepted them as part of His life. During that crucial last evening in the Garden when His disciples failed to stand with Him even one hour in prayer, He did not condemn them. Jesus expressed His disappointment and sadness, then walked on toward the cross where He would suffer the ultimate in loss.

Gethsemane reveals as perhaps no other place the true manhood of Jesus. Not in the historian's annals or realm of fiction can anything equal the degradation of that unholy trial. Hoping to find a charge against the Prisoner, they used base devices and illegal tricks to secure a guilty verdict to ensure the death penalty.[5] While Jesus did never sin, He was not an automatically programmed robot. He faced painful choices between obedience and disobedience.[6] "He came unto His own, and His own received Him not" (Jn. 1:11 KJV). Those of us who have suffered great loss can "feel" with Jesus our Savior and Lord. But never can we *know* the loneliness, despair, and sadness in His dark hour of Gethsemane. The ultimate sadness.

Christ knew the cross was only hours away. Christ knew His disciples and close friends would desert Him, that He would be emotionally separated from His Heavenly Father. Even though that separation was unavoidable, Jesus was experiencing overwhelming torment from the prospect of dying for your and my sins.[7] He was trying to deal with His torment in that crucial hour and at the same time cope with ultimate loss. Jesus was feeling depressed and extreme sadness; yet, had He not, He could not now relate to us in our times of loss. But, He walked on. Jesus triumphed over the evil one, showing us how to walk through extreme sadness and depression during times of loss.

First, Jesus chose to be with others during a time of great loss. He neither denied His feelings nor withdrew from others.

Second, Jesus revealed His innermost feelings. He risked being vulnerable even in the face of being rejected.

Third, Jesus asked His closest friends for emotional support. He didn't hesitate to give others the opportunity to minister to Him, although they failed to do so.[8] His practical and helpful model is available for each of us to connect with during times of loss.

Summarizing Our Thoughts on Jesus and Loss and Feeling Sad

"So what?" So what that Jesus felt sad during times of loss? How can that help you during your times of loss and sadness? Do you resist asking and letting others reach out to you in time of need? Consider Jesus' healthy emotional response model. Like Christ did, you can choose to be with others during a time of great loss. You need not deny your feelings nor withdraw from others. Like Christ did, you can reveal your innermost feelings to those whom you trust. You need not fear the risk of being vulnerable, even in the face of being rejected. Like Christ did, you can ask your closest friends for emotional support. You need not hesitate to give others the opportunity to minister to you although they may fail to do so. You can learn to ask and allow others to reach out to you by connecting with Jesus' balanced, healthy model of dealing with loss and sadness. In the next chapter, we will discover why Jesus felt sorrow during times of loss.

Chapter Twenty-seven

Jesus Felt Sorrow During Times of Loss

And taking with Him Peter
and the two sons of Zebedee,
[Jesus]...said to them...
I am almost dying of sorrow....

Matthew 26:37-38 AMP

"Whatever you have planned, now is the time to put it into action" (Jn. 13:27 par.). Judas Iscariot alone understood Jesus' words. In that decisive instant, Judas decided to help betray Jesus and the devil entered him. Shortly before that decision, Jesus had beautifully modeled His servant role by washing the feet of each disciple. Washing their feet typified the need of our soul's daily purification from the travel stains of life using Scripture and prayer.[1] Sadly, this truth escaped Judas. He left immediately to set in motion the darkest of treachery against that One whom "he loved not at all." Later, Jesus and His faithful 11 left the Upper Chamber. The moon's soft light guided them through the dark Kidron valley, over the Kidron brook, to the lower western slope of Mount Olive.[2] Since the group had not understood Christ's instructions to Judas, they did not hold a clear mental picture of why Jesus was taking them to Gethsemane. Sleepy eyes hid from them an agonizing sorrow spreading over Christ's moonlit face. Shortly, they would understand the special moment when a woman poured her costly perfume over Christ, preparing Him for burial. From Judas Iscariot's most dastardly act they would slowly understand Jesus' need for them to watch and pray with Him in His time of sorrow.[3]

Feeling Sorrow During Times of Loss

Since the time Jesus walked this earth with His healthy emotional responses, most of us have failed to discover and connect with those models.

As a result, there is a widespread misunderstanding about feeling sincere sorrow during times of loss.[4] This may account for those Christians who cannot let themselves grieve during loss. Regardless of the loss, if we don't walk through a time of grieving and feeling sorrow, an anger leading to depression can develop. Joni Eareckson Tada and former Senator Bob Dole have shared about the long months, even years, needed for healing and recovery from their physical and emotional losses.[5] Many "feel" with them while others seem to think they should have denied their loss and walked on as though nothing debilitating had changed their bodies. People taking this attitude fail to take time for a healthy sorrow and want others to do the same, regardless of emotional destruction to their lives or relationships. Jesus Christ did not deny His emotional pain. He modeled the importance of recognizing loss while walking through a time of sorrow.

Coping With Sorrow and Loss in Childhood

As a result of being born with a hip problem, before age two Jacquie had to spend one year in a hospital. Her legs were encased with casts and had to be elevated most of the time. This usually kept the two-year-old on her back, which interfered with normal activities and playing time. She had one sister a little older than her. During that one-year hospital stay, her baby brother was born. Since her father didn't like hospitals and worked long, erratic hours as a truck driver, he failed to visit her during that scary, sorrowful year. Jacquie thought her father hadn't come because he didn't love her.

Because of hospital regulations, Jacquie's mom could only visit her for two hours on Sunday afternoons. Her mother lived quite some distance away; to get to the hospital, she travelled by city bus from Minneapolis to St. Paul. Then, in order to finish the trip, she had to walk a mile because of lacking taxi money. Jacquie remembers her mom only missing one Sunday, and that was when the little brother was born. Each Sunday Jacquie's mother brought books, crayons, and games. To help them play together better, a nurse would turn Jacquie onto her stomach. After a few weeks, someone complained that other children didn't receive that kind of attention so her mom was told to stop bringing toys. However, she found ways to take in a few unnoticed.

On returning home from the one-year hospital confinement, Jacquie felt like a stranger with her family and had to go through a period of readjusting to them. Adding to the overall stress, she had to wear different types of leg braces off and on for about 12 more years. Besides physical pain, there was emotional pain with which to try and cope. Kids made fun of Jacquie's braces and called her names. In order to support her legs and braces, she had to wear high-top white leather shoes. Because they looked different from shoes worn by other children Jacquie's age—to her they looked like baby shoes—she felt others were treating her like a baby. The name calling, odd-looking shoes, and braces served to only make her more determined to overcome her emotional and physical losses. The doctor had said "No" to certain activities; but to prove to other children she wasn't helpless, Jacquie ignored his limitation. While wearing braces she found ways and energy to run, roller-skate, or jump rope.

When her braces had to be repaired, Jacquie had a little red wagon in which to ride. During her years of braces, she had to return to the hospital twice for a month's reevaluation time. She never knew how nurses would respond to her particular needs. One of those times she contracted chicken pox and had to be quarantined. But no one explained to her why she had to be closed off from everyone. Those were very lonely and sorrowful times. Jacquie also had to learn how to deal with comments like, "Just be tough. There are those who are worse off than you." Such words helped mold her personality with a false guilt that taught Jacquie to deny her pain. At the same time, she learned a pseudo responsibility for trying to "fix" others, but could not feel compassion with them because she was denying her own needs.

Since then, Jacquie has learned much about herself, others, and her Heavenly Father. She sees Him as "a Good Dad" with unconditional love for her. This helps her to be honest and vulnerable with God. She has learned it's okay to express her anger to God. However, when Jacquie relates to Him in impatience or disrespect she confesses that immediately. Through such openness with God, her "Good Dad," she is freed to become that person He designed her to be. Jacquie believes God is using her painful childhood for good, to bring emotional and spiritual maturity. Her fear of "messing up" is gone; but if she does, Jacquie knows He forgives. She continues to learn and grow rather than crawl into an emotional hole as she did in the past. Jacquie also continues to free herself from the myth that she has to "fix" her or others' problems. She knows that Jesus Christ is the source and power we go to in times of sorrow and loss. Jesus is helping her turn sorrow and loss into joy and gain.

Coping With Sorrow and Loss in Adulthood

For some of us, adulthood began when we were children. This was true for Ann in many ways. At age four she suffered the loss of her father through an electrical accident. After his death, Ann's mother decided they needed to move. So they moved to the state where Ann's father and mother had grown up. That meant the loss of friends and other relationships. However, Ann was not able to begin her grieving process until years later when her older brother was killed in the line of duty. Her brother's unexpected death came at the same time her marriage was falling apart. Ann didn't want a divorce, but her spouse didn't consider that. The emotional fallout of her father's death combined with the loss of a beloved brother and an unwanted divorce hovered over her like a dark cloud. Since she couldn't grieve all three at the same time, she has tried to walk—at times crawl—through the "maze of sorrow" one turn at a time.

Ann had moved many times and each time meant walking through the loss of dear friends and emotional ties. Now, because of the divorce, another move was added to Ann's "maze." A job change took her to another part of the state where she was living. Once again Ann felt the sorrow of losing friends and emotional ties. In the midst of trying to cope with the fallout of heavy emotional losses, she felt the reality weight of identity crises. Ann has walked in and out of different identities since her adulthood began as a child. The greatest help during these times is the knowledge and confidence that Jesus Christ through the Holy Spirit lives within her. The Lord God is very important to Ann, helping her continue in life when at times she wants to quit. There have always been special friends. But next to God, the greatest strength came from her mother. Some years after her divorce and her brother's death, Ann decided to move again. She knew another move would again involve giving up friends and emotional ties; but her mom's health was deteriorating. Ann said, "Mom had always been there for me and I wanted to live in the same town to be there for her."

Living close to her mother felt rewarding for Ann in many ways. It was the area where she had grown up, her new job gave some challenge, and the church provided opportunity for spiritual growth. Ann was able to once again develop close friends who were there for her when that "unwanted day" arrived. Six years after that move, Ann's mother died from congestive heart failure. That was two years ago. Ann's tears ran freely as she talked about the mother who meant so very much to her—the one who had tried to help fill some of Ann's emptiness caused by continual emotional loss.

Some, looking on from the outside, would envy Ann. Despite losing her father at a young age, Ann felt happy growing up. She had friends, attended a well-known university, and has had no real problems the past 25 years getting meaningful employment as a nurse. But, few know about the continual emotional losses which fill her slow-walking maze. A short time before this chapter went to print, Ann suffered another great loss. A dear friend, suffering from depression, could not accept others' comfort and ended her life. Trying to cope with this latest sorrow, Ann still desires to be able to reach out and help others during their emotional pain and loss. She believes that is one way Jesus Christ can continue to turn her losses into gain.

Jesus Christ and Loss and Feeling Sorrow

Jesus was a Man of sorrow; He was acquainted with the grief of being despised and rejected by His very own people. He knew the sorrow of being abandoned by His beloved disciples whom He had chosen, trained, lived with, and worked with so closely for three years. He knew the sorrow of watching those around Him walking in sin. He knew the sorrow of watching death's destructive work on His created, loved humanity. He knew the emotional pain of grieving with others in their pain, for their loss was also His loss. He knew the deep sorrow of preparing Himself for the cross, and its indescribable physical pain.

Yet, despite His sorrows, Jesus Christ was not the "picture" of an unhappy person. It does not matter that we find no Scriptural evidence of a smiling face. It matters not that Scripture doesn't record laughter.[6] Beneath His heavy weight of sorrow oozed joy, peace, love, gladness, and rejoicing in the Holy Spirit. These healthy emotions came from knowing the "always" presence of His Father and the assurance that He was doing His Father's work. Part of that work was modeling for us how to live and function under the heavy burden of sorrow and loss.

First, Jesus chose to be with close, trusted friends during times of great loss. He did not withdraw from others but sought their fellowship.

Second, Jesus shared His true feelings with His friends. Even in the face of being misunderstood or rejected, He risked being vulnerable with those trusted few.

Third, Jesus asked emotional and prayerful support from those with whom He wanted fellowship. Although they failed Him, He didn't hesitate to give them opportunity to minister to Him.[7] This helpful and practical model is available for you and me to use during times of loss.

Summarizing Our Thoughts on Jesus and Loss and Feeling Sorrow

"So what?" So what that Jesus felt sorrow during times of loss? How can that help you during your times of loss and sorrow? Do you have difficulty sharing with others and allowing them to encourage you during sorrow? If so, like Jesus did, you can choose to be with close, trusted friends during times of loss. You need not withdraw from others; you can accept their friendship. Like Jesus, you can share your true feelings with those whom you trust. You need not fear being misunderstood or rejected if you will allow Jesus Christ to help you risk being vulnerable with a few trusted friends or family members. Like Christ did, you can ask emotional support of those from whom you have fellowship. Although others (including us) are not without fault, you can give them opportunity to reach out to you. But remember, it's your responsibility to discover and connect with Jesus Christ's balanced, healthy model of dealing with loss and sorrow. In the next chapter, we will discover why Jesus wept during times of loss.

Chapter Twenty-eight

Jesus Wept
During
Times of Loss

..."Where have you laid [Lazarus]?"
They said to Him,
"Lord, come and see."
Jesus wept.

John 11:34-35

"Martha, Mary, listen to Me. Lazarus will return to physical life because of Me. I am the resurrection and the life—not time, not place" (Jn. 11:25 par.). Jesus waited until Rabbinic directions for accompanying the dead were carried out for His friend Lazarus before going to Bethany. Because of Lazarus' position in the community his body was not put in a cemetery but rather in a private tomb in some cave, probably located in one of the local gardens. Despite a close relationship with Jesus, this family of three had evidently been in good standing in the synagogue. The mark of sorrow, respect, and sympathy had been shown by friends in their district and neighboring Jerusalem. This show of kindness for the family to honor their dead was very comforting. These friends were in the fourth day of sharing demonstrations of grief with Mary and Martha when Jesus and His disciples arrived.[1]

Since the mourning period would last for 30 days, the bereaved sisters were not surprised to see Jesus and His disciples on that fourth day. In their voices, Jesus could hear the bewilderment and betrayal they felt because He had not come before Lazarus died. Jesus understood the sisters' confusion and anger for He also felt anger; actually He raged in His insides. But His "irrepressible anger" was toward the unnaturalness and evil of death, and him who has the power of death; the one whom He came to destroy. At that moment, His anger was manifested as tears. Because of emotional devastation forced on Mary and Martha when the enemy *death* took their beloved Lazarus, "Jesus wept" with them. On this day, they could not understand that the "resurrection and life" are not special gifts to humanity but literally Jesus Christ Himself as He did God's will. This was certainly new "resurrection" teaching.[2] It was Christ's purpose and meaning for raising Lazarus back to physical life.[3] "One loud command spoken into that silence; one loud call to that sleeper; one flash of God's Own Light into that darkness, and the wheels of life again moved at the outgoing of The Life."[4] The weeping and mourning turned into instant joy instead of loss.

Feeling the Need to Weep During Times of Loss

Christ's balanced life shows us that weeping during times of loss is normal and emotionally healthy. Christ's emotional responses also show us different levels of feelings and weeping. When Jesus wept with Mary and Martha, His tears flowed from having to observe the emotional dev-astation and physical deterioration caused by death.[5] His tears were more of anger at death than feeling sympathy. Most of us have probably felt *anger* with death. Likewise, with the same type of experience we will walk through loss at different emotional levels according to personality and background. When Jane was 12, her 18-year-old brother died from an ac-cident. She had loved him and at first cried openly. But after her grand-mother said she should not cry and two friends laughed about her crying at the funeral, her tears dried. These unkind messages told her she couldn't feel healthy emotional responses in times of loss. Jane deeply feels loss, but it's still difficult sometimes for her tears to flow freely in front of oth-ers. Instead of feeling sincere sadness, at times she feels anger over the cir-cumstances. We remain more physically, emotionally, and spiritually healthy by following Christ's example of weeping openly during times of loss.

Coping With Weeping and Childhood Loss

Most of us can probably point to different types of loss in our child-hood. But Alan's childhood was more severe than the average. While a baby and ending at about age three, he suffered the evils of satanic ritual abuse from next-door neighbors without his parents' knowledge or con-sent. As a toddler, his parents began to see unusual behavior for a child that age. They couldn't understand why he suffered from many irrational fears their other children had not expressed. At times, for no apparent rea-son, he would start weeping like he felt frightened. While tears washed his face a parent would try to console him. After Alan's family and he moved to another town, his fears seemed to have less control over him. Years later they would realize that those irrational fears had actually frozen inside his brain to dribble out in the teenage years.

His 6-foot, 3-inch height and 165-pound weight could have been an asset in playing high school football and basketball. Instead, Alan found he could not endure the coaches' cursing and yelling so he withdrew from all competitive sports. Music felt safer. He transferred his talented energy to writing music and overseeing a Christian rock band until about age 20. At the same time, his inside fears were growing stronger on the outside. In the evenings, Alan couldn't understand why going into the dark attached garage to practice music sent shivers of fear over him.

The summer he was 17, he suffered an emotional breakdown and a second at 23. Until memories of satanic ritual abuse (SRA) started surfacing in his mid-twenties, neither he nor his family or counselor realized the basis of fears or emotional attacks suffered since a toddler. As memories surfaced of loud voices screaming at him during times of torment, Alan understood why he couldn't endure the coaches' yelling. Remembering bad things done to him in the dark showed him why the dark garage had felt so scary. After many years of spiritual and emotional healing, Alan reached an acceptance of God's sovereignty in regards to his childhood loss of innocence, safety, trust, and security. In his marriage, family, relationships, and service to the Lord, God continues to turn his losses into gain.[6]

Coping With Weeping and Adulthood Loss

Adulthood for Diana has been similar to her childhood in that loss and weeping have described most of Diana's 39 years. As young as 17, she married a 21-year-old young man who said God wanted him to preach. Diana eagerly used her many talents and spiritual gifts in supporting her husband's call. In less than six years they had three children. Along with her many in-house and parenting responsibilities, Diana worked outside the house to help supplement her husband's salary. Somehow, she managed to attend college and receive a teaching degree. After about 15 years her husband left the pastorate, took a truck-driving job, and became overly friendly with a woman who worked at one of his regular stops. One night, he shocked Diana by telling of the affair that he planned to continue. She spent that night weeping. After many months of the marriage going from bad to worst, Diana moved herself and the children. They had gone from a two-parent, two-salary household to a one-parent, one-salary household. Their whole livelihood rested on her petite five-foot, two-inch determined commitment.

Two years later, the school principal called Diana from her classroom. She was told that two of her teenagers had been hospitalized from a serious car accident. Pastors and friends waited for her at the hospital. Tim and Rebecca were in the same ICU only feet apart; neither was expected to live. Since doctors said Tim was in the worst condition, Diana sat beside him hours on end—holding his hand. Once she asked nurses to adjust the many tubes connecting Tim to life machines so she could cuddle him in her arms. Some hours later, Tim died. Rebecca was in the rehabilitation center for a year, and Diana took a leave of absence from teaching to be with her. Rebecca had to use a wheelchair when she came home. Diana was hospitalized for a while from physical and emotional exhaustion from lifting and helping Rebecca.

In less than a year, Diana's second husband died from a heart attack. Only two years earlier, her stepmother and grandmother had died. Saying good-bye to loved ones began for Diana as a child when she said good-bye to her mother because of divorce. By devious means, Diana's alcoholic father gained custody over her and a younger sister. Many times, defying the Court, he refused to allow her mother to visit. He told the girls their mother was bad and that she didn't want to see them. After many months they began to believe the lies. As teenagers they learned about their mother's love for them and their father's cruelty to her. Their stepmother and father had functioned by mood swings. At times the girls were treated with kindness and at other times they were beaten. Although cuts and bruises were seen by school teachers, nothing was done to help Diana and her sister. The only comfort they felt was from their own weeping and tears.

From her youth Diana has remained faithful in her commitment to Christ and the church family. Despite years of emotional pain and loss, her face radiates a peace that comes only from faith in Jesus Christ. "I know who I am in Christ and I can operate only through His power," are Diana's words. She knows as long as we live on this earth that "bad things will happen to good people." Her inner strength comes from the Holy Spirit, God's Word, prayer, and trusting in God's sovereignty. About the same time that doctors told Diana that Tim was brain-dead, a double rainbow was seen at their hometown Christian university. Someone took a picture of it and a copy hangs on Diana's living room wall. Many young people from their church believed the rainbow was God's sign that Tim stood in His presence. Diana has learned of individuals who have since believed in Christ as a result of Tim's death. Over two years later, Rebecca has not yet fully recovered. While Diana knows her weeping and loss have not ended, she hopes and trusts in Jesus Christ who is turning her losses into gain.

Jesus Christ and Feeling Loss and Weeping

Jesus didn't try to deny or downplay the sisters' grief by saying they should not weep or wail. Jesus respected their need to grieve and receive emotional support. He wept with them as though a "storm of wrath" swept over Him. He mingled tears of sympathy and irrepressible anger with His beloved friends. Jesus burned against death with rage for what He saw it doing to His precious created beings. Other evils also enraged Christ. He rebuked a fever, the wind, the sea, and unclean spirits because each tormented mankind. He chided and cast out demons because of "the tyrannous evil which they were working upon their victims." His displeasure that He directed toward the malignant power behind these manifestations was the same that He conquered at Lazarus' tomb.[7] Jesus still feels with His own during their times of oppression, and modeled how to weep during times of loss.

First, Jesus listened to the whole story. He knew the importance of hearing the facts before responding.

Second, Jesus was moved inwardly with others during their time of loss. He did not pretend to be in touch with their emotional needs; He felt with and for them.

Third, Jesus wept openly with others. His feelings were real; He did not mask or fake an emotional response in their presence.[8] This model is ours for the developing.

Summarizing Our Thoughts on Jesus and Loss and Weeping

"So what?" So what that Jesus wept during times of loss? What does this mean to you? Do you have difficulty weeping with and for others? Like Jesus, learn to listen to the whole story; get the facts before responding. Like Jesus did, let your insides be moved with others during their time of loss. Don't pretend to be in touch with their emotional needs, just allow yourself to *feel* with and for them. Like Jesus did, weep openly with others when that's appropriate. Let your feelings be real; do not mask or fake an emotional response in the presence of others. "Feeling" with hurting others may be difficult if this isn't your practice. But you can study about Jesus' emotional responses; you can learn to connect with His emotions; you can use the Holy Spirit's power to help you feel your losses and feel with others during their times of loss. In the next chapter, we will discover why Jesus felt physical hunger while moving through life.

Chapter Twenty-nine

Jesus Felt Hunger
While
Moving Through Life

Then Jesus was led up by the Spirit
into the wilderness to be tempted by the devil.
And after He had fasted forty days and forty nights,
He then became hungry.

Matthew 4:1-2

"My Son, My Beloved, in Whom I delight," proclaimed our Holy Father from the heavens (Mt. 3:17 AMP). After John the Baptist loudly protested of his unworthiness to baptize Jesus, he agreed to do so in the river Jordan. In the bodily form of a dove, the Holy Spirit descended and alighted on Jesus as He came out of the water. Landing lightly on the wet shoulder of Jesus, the "Spirit-dove" signified God's seal of approval. His baptism was the first step in beginning a stormy earthly ministry. Hardly before His clothes were dry, the Holy Spirit took Jesus into the desert wilderness of Quarantania.[1] The Holy Spirit took the Beloved Son there to school and prepare Him for His long-awaited Life business. Some 18 years had passed since Jesus told Mary and Joseph He needed to be about His Father's business.[2] Although that concentrated and ongoing schooling time is a fuzzy picture for us, we can see that He learned *"when* His business was to commence, and *how* it would be done."[3] Why Scripture does not describe that training period remains a mystery. But after going without eating solid food for 40 days and nights, Jesus felt faint with hunger.[4]

Satisfying One's Physical Hunger Need

Some of those among us called "work-a-holics" might look at Christ's intense training time and His failure to eat solid food to okay their unhealthy behavior of ongoing overcommitments and overworking. But I remind them that Christ not taking time to eat food was just a one-time experience rather than an ongoing behavior. Scripture doesn't generously describe whether His activity required much energy during those days. Going without solid food for more than a month, however, depletes one's energy level. Yet, we can assume there were plants like dessert cactus fruit from which Christ could get a liquid nourishment to provide some strength. Nevertheless, since Jesus had not eaten solid food during the 40 days and nights, He felt weak and hungry.

One sign of physical life is the feeling of hunger. To satisfy the feeling of hunger is not sin, but satisfying hunger in the wrong way can be sin. The devil chose that opportunity to attack and to take advantage of Jesus. Satan knew God had given mankind a common practice of obtaining food by hard work and faith. After the devil saw that Jesus was hungry, he severely tempted the God-man to get food by an uncalled-for means. Lucifer wanted Christ to turn from God and bow down in worship to him. That's why he urged Jesus to get food by commanding stones into bread. This means of getting food was wrong by God's standards because it was prideful self-assertion. The devil was pressuring Christ to prove He was the Son of God by using an abnormal and spectacular means to satisfy His hunger feelings.[5]

Angelic Help With Hunger Feelings While Moving Through Life

Jesus refused to turn the rocks into bread, for He knew this would have been acting from prideful self-assertion and distrust. Such uncalled-for means in satisfying His normal hunger feelings would have denied rather than affirmed His Sonship.[6] His choice showed us the importance of using God's common practice of hard work and faith to obtain our food, letting others help in time of need, and helping others in their need. Jesus refused to act from a prideful self-assertion and His Holy Father honored Him with provisions by angels. Before Jesus came to earth as the God-man, He had authority over angels, God's ministering spirits. Now they were gladly serving Him and ministering to His needs during a time of great weariness from being tempted and weakness from physical hunger.

Both good and evil angels hold our attention again after many seasons of almost silence. Estimates say that in the United States alone there are 200,000 witches. Some hotels and conventions hire psychics to entertain guests. Satanism philosophy is promoted by the lyrics of rock music groups. "Black magic and voodooism have long been in existence, and religious groups, such as Santeria, are seeking approval for animal sacrifices under the guise of freedom of religion."[7] A recent poll in *Time* Magazine shows that 69 percent of Americans believe in angels and 46 percent believe in a personal guardian angel.[8] Believing the Bible helps us believe in angels and expect powerful, good angels to accompany us through life experiences under God's guidance.

> "The empire of angels is as vast as God's creation...They crisscross the Old and New Testaments, being mentioned directly or indirectly nearly 300 times...It seems that angels have the ability to change their appearance and shuttle in a flash from the capital glory of heaven to earth and back again...they do not possess physical bodies, although they may take on physical bodies when God appoints them to special tasks."[9]

Angels may choose to become visible to carry out an assignment from God. But normally we don't see them, just as we don't see the electricity that flows through copper wiring. Scripture assures "us that there is a world of intelligent, powerful, invisible creatures about us and above us that warrants our prayerful and careful study."[10] God's ministering spirits cannot and do not indwell us; they cannot convict us of sin; they do not guide us into Truth nor can they empower or change us. We do not pray to or worship angels. God only is worthy of praise (see Ps. 18:3). While angels have emotions and can speak, they never draw attention to themselves. They were created to give glory to God and to serve Him. They "are privileged, limited, and responsible" to God in all things.[11] Although we may ask God to provide an angel's help, the decision is His to determine whether our request is an actual need. God at times sends angelic help without our asking as He did in meeting Jesus' need for rest and food.

Helping Those Feeling Hunger While Moving Through Life

There are times when Jane and I have the opportunity to provide help for those in need. Both of us have been approached by those feeling hunger. We try to minister to them as we would like others to minister to us; and we give as unto the Lord, in Jesus' name. Once when a woman asked Jane for money, she offered to buy her lunch instead and the young woman accepted. Some weeks later, at another fast-food chain, that same woman approached Jane for another meal. This time, after they ate, Jane drove her home. Later, Jane felt compelled to take frozen food from our freezer to this woman and her family. When the young woman saw the food, she reacted in anger; she had wanted money to help her with a habit. This is why Jane and I buy or give food rather than money to a stranger.

About six o'clock one morning Jane and I were entering a Denny's. A man asked me if I would buy him and his wife breakfast. I said, "Sure, just go in and order whatever you want." Inside the restaurant I asked the cashier to put on my bill whatever the next couple coming through the door would order. Since Jane and I had started our trip at four a.m., we were tired and not very alert. After we finished eating, Jane talked with the couple while I paid the bill and then we went to our car. Another couple came out of the restaurant and thanked me for breakfast. They were amazed that a stranger would pay for their meal. We felt puzzled by their words but just thought they had seen me pay for the other couple's breakfast. When the Visa bill came with our moving expenses, we were shocked to see a $36.50 charge for breakfast. Rehashing that morning at Denny's, we realized I had not clearly described my intentions or clearly checked the bill. Evidently the cashier thought I intended to pay for each couple that came in. After the shock wore off, we rejoiced that our eating time had been short that morning. Otherwise other couples "not in need" would have received a free breakfast.

For several years, both Jane and I enjoyed the privilege of giving money for food to the Los Angeles Mission especially at Easter, Thanksgiving, and Christmas. Along with hundreds of others, we helped serve meals to between 3,000 and 5,000 homeless at those times. The city of Los Angeles gives permission each season to block off a street for a day where faithful volunteers set up and decorate hundreds of tables. Catering trucks keep the food hot while volunteers keep food coming to the serving line, then others spoon the food onto white Styrofoam plates carried by the hungry. At Christmas time gift bags filled with practical items like deodorant, toothpaste, toothbrushes, and socks were given to each person. Serving was tiring but it was very rewarding to see hungry children and adults eating nutritious food given and served in Jesus' name.

Jesus Christ and Life and Feeling Physical Hunger

While moving through life, Jesus not only felt hunger He helped many who also felt hunger. Because Jesus knew what physical hunger felt like and because He was filled with compassion, He wanted to reach out to those in need. Yet, it's evident from Scripture that Jesus did not personally fill every hungry stomach. He wanted mankind to share His compassion and reach out to each other. Today, every hungry stomach is not filled because a large portion of us Christians do not share compassion with the legitimately hungry. One source says that every day there are between 12 million to 20 million empty stomachs.[12] A portion of those figures fall under the type of malnutrition that comes from consistently eating junk food rather than lacking funds for nutritious food. But, figures in the millions are so overwhelming that we must break them down into individuals from our hometown in order to become aware of the true hunger problem.

Jesus did that. His disciples felt overwhelmed at Christ's suggestion of feeding the thousands who had come to hear Him preach. But He simply told them to look around for what food they already had and bring it to Him. He took the small amount of fish and bread they found, told the people to sit down in groups of 50 and 100, and asked His Heavenly Father to bless the food. Then Jesus broke the loaves and fishes, started putting them into the disciples' baskets, and they started giving from the baskets to those thousands. When the thousands had satisfied their hunger, there were 12 remaining full baskets to feed other hungry stomachs (see Mk. 6:33-44; Mt. 14:13-21). God does not use angels to do what He calls us to do.

There are several New Testament references to Christ and feeding the hungry. At times He's talking about feeding the spiritually hungry. But Jesus tells His men clearly that when they feed, clothe, or visit the sick or others in need, their activities are never to be done in a prideful self-assertion. They are to be done as unto Him and for the Holy Father's glory. Whether Jesus felt hungry or whether He was feeding the hungry, we have His model to follow. This sensible model from Christ is ours for the using.

First, Jesus did not hesitate to make His physical needs known in a discreet way. He spoke about them to friends because He evidently wanted them known.

Second, Jesus did not behave in prideful self-assertion. He used God's common practice of work and faith for food, whether it was for others' hunger or His own hunger.

Third, Jesus asked His Heavenly Father to bless His efforts to get food. He did not work independently of God or of others; He worked interdependently with them.[13]

Summarizing Our Thoughts on Jesus and Life and Feeling Hunger

"So what?" So what that Jesus felt hungry while moving through life? Whether or not you have known hunger or know those who have, how can the model of Jesus affect your life for good? Like Jesus, you need not hesitate to make your needs known in a discreet way. He didn't pretend all was okay when it was not, and spoke about it to friends. Like Jesus, don't behave in prideful self-assertion. You can use God's common practice of work and faith for food, whether it is for others' hunger or your own. Like Jesus, ask your Heavenly Father to bless your efforts to get food. Don't work independently of God or others; work interdependently with them. It's your responsibility to connect with Jesus Christ's practical model so He can help in your times of need. In the next chapter we will discover why Jesus felt weary and thirsty while moving through life.

Chapter Thirty

Jesus Felt Weary and Thirsty
While
Moving Through Life

....Jesus therefore,
being wearied from His journey,
was sitting thus by [Jacob's] well....
After this, Jesus, knowing that all things
had already been accomplished...said,
"I am thirsty."

John 4:6; 19:28

"Sir, you look and sound like a Jew. Why do you ask a drink of water from me—a Samaritan woman, hated by Your people?" (Jn. 4:9 par.) Jesus needed rest and water; she needed privacy. Both knew that "noon" was not the usual time for women to draw water from Jacob's 9-foot wide, 100-foot deep well.[1] She may have chosen that time in order to avoid the village women's stares and unkind words. Her multiple marriages, plus living with a man outside of marriage, was this woman's public identity. Her pattern of emotional instability gives one reason to wonder if she had suffered sexual violations as a child. It's evident she lived under a burden of shame, which Jesus wanted to release her from and replace with eternal Living Water. Unkindness or disrespect from Jesus to women is not found in Scripture. On this hot day, accepting love and compassion flowed freely from Jesus to the woman. To her uneducated mind He patiently explained the reality of a coming Messiah.[2] Moving from curious to serious interest, she responded to His kind and respectful manner.[3] When Jesus told the woman about her past five husbands and present live-in, she "saw" His Deity. After she said, "I believe that Messiah, the Christ, is coming," Jesus answered, "I am He" (Jn. 4:25-26 par.). He gave Living Water to a shame-burdened woman and no longer felt weary or thirsty.[4]

Dealing With the Stress of Thirst and Weariness

Busyness—not necessarily serving—has so taken us over than even young children speak of "being bored" if they aren't constantly busy. Over half of all women today live as single, yet a large portion of them are parents. Yet, in most cases, single moms have the full responsibility of raising their children.[5] The father either forgets his children or spends little time with them as he reinvents another family. With computers taking over more jobs, we're not only dependent on them but most age levels are now required to learn how to operate them. Since everyone is not "computer happy" this is adding additional emotional stress to our already overburdened society. Many men and women have had to retrain for other types of jobs after a computer stole theirs. Regardless of whether children are "computer happy," they are required to produce school assignments on a computer. Like with Jesus and the Samaritan woman, we feel weary and thirsty because of busyness.

The Reality of Moving Through Life With a Thirsty, Weary Busyness

Often I forget about Christ's model of taking His disciples to a quiet place to rest (see Mk. 6:30-32). I get so involved with serving others and making a living, hurrying here and there, that *busyness* overwhelms me. Without recognizing it, I've allowed "hurry sickness" to take me over. I find myself in a cycle of "go, go, go," without the inner strength to stop. I overcommit, neglect time for my family, and forget that my self-esteem doesn't rest on busyness. When we've been taken over by hurry sickness, an anticipation of getting some reward replaces the original enjoyment for responsibilities or serving.[6] That is when we are faced with the desperate need to replace our thirsty weariness with planned relaxation and rest. Since Jesus saw the importance of taking time away from His busy life for rest, we can do so also and without false guilt.

Many times a hurry sickness is preceded by the **addiction** of "doing for others." Addictions are not just alcohol or drug related; they are work, people, and loss related. We might describe addiction as something or someone we have allowed to become number one in our lives, rather than Jesus Christ. By this I mean that we give more mental, emotional, and spiritual space to the something or someone than we give to the Lord. When we fail to keep a balance in our work hours, church activities, relationships, and family commitments, busyness rather than the Holy Spirit will control us. Like with the Samaritan woman, each of us know people who are hard to deal with, create splitting headaches, and cause upset stomachs. We must interact with them at work, church, parties, and home. But when we suffer from hurry sickness or addiction, we also relate to others from a thirsty weariness, causing them and us emotional harm.

One Example of Moving Through Life With a Thirsty, Weary Busyness

Joy Marie is a friend of ours. She grew up in a home with legalistic thinking and acting parents. Her father was cordial and friendly to strangers and employees, but he was often very harsh at home. His anger level was always high, and Marie never knew how to avoid causing an explosion. She seemed to have the knack of saying the wrong thing at the wrong time, bringing his wrath down upon her body. At times she would hide where it seemed safe, hoping to escape his verbal and physical abuse for a few hours. One evening in her mid-teen years she needed safety and went to her church. After being raped by the youth pastor, Marie discovered her church was not safe either. Because Marie's parents would blame her rather than console her, she didn't tell them. The pastor was never confronted or disciplined for his sin, and no one ministered to Marie in her physical and emotional pain of shame.

Many years passed before she could talk about those horrid growing-up years. By that time, her mind was filled with accusing and condemning lies of the devil. She had come to believe that her behavior was to blame for those uncalled-for violations. After college, she taught in elementary education at a Christian-run school. After several years of teaching with an excellent record, she was wrongfully fired because of a principal's misconduct. Marie was a friend of her pastor and his family at that time and thought he was trustworthy. Going to him for counsel and consolation should have been safe. But to her horror and dismay, once again her personal boundaries were crossed by a pastor. Marie realized she was living with a thirsty weariness.

From teaching she went into banking and before long had again established an excellent work record. In reality, Marie had turned to *busyness* trying to gain mental and emotional sanity. She took on a pattern of overwork, trying to prove to others that she is good enough. Marie consistently overworks, spending long hours each week for which she isn't paid. In addition, she enrolls in several classes at a local college each semester and is never satisfied with a grade less than an "A." This keeps her mind occupied and provides a good reason for not being available to socialize.

Her addiction to work, however, has caused serious physical problems. Three times Marie has battled cancer. These have been physically and emotionally weary, thirsty times because of the side effects of chemotherapy. Among others, it causes extreme loss of hair necessitating the patient to wear a wig. Through all the suffering in moving through chemotherapy, Marie faithfully kept going to work. Fearing their rejection, several years passed before Marie found the courage to tell her parents about the cancer. While they have helped some financially, their response has not been very sympathetic. This relationship adds another reason why Marie has such a difficult time trusting God or others. Most of the uncalled-for emotional damage forced on her came from "Christians." Although Marie goes to church, it remains a struggle for her after all these years. One family in particular has "adopted" Marie. They encourage her to slow down, let go of overwork, and let go of a thirsty weariness.

Jesus Christ and Feeling Weary and Thirsty

Scripture shows that the God-man felt weary and thirsty while moving through life. Just as He was Deity, He was also humanity. He had the same needs as you and I to eat, work, pray, drink, and sleep. Because of His humanity, He knew what it was to be "weary"; yet His weariness was not **of** well doing but **in** well doing.[7] He felt the most extreme thirst when He hung and suffered on the cross. Jesus felt the most extreme weariness after going 40 days without solid food when the devil attacked and tempted Him. Christ did not live in a phantom body that could not feel pain; His bodily suffering was real.[8] That's why He can and does "feel" with us in our weary and thirsty times. Jesus honored His need for physical rest and fresh water, but those needs didn't keep Him from reaching out in *agape* love and receiving a shame-burdened woman. He had a Divine appointment to go through Samaria to share His eternal Living Water. In answering that driving motivation, He actually met His feelings of tiredness and thirst.

Christ's concern for physical weariness and thirst was balanced with His concern for spiritual weariness and thirst. Just as He patiently taught the unlearned Samaritan woman, He patiently teaches us. Just as He satisfied her spiritually weary and thirsty needs, He eagerly satisfies our spiritual weariness and thirst. Just as He honored and satisfied His feelings of weariness and thirst, He willingly satisfies our physical feelings of weariness and thirst. Christ showed us how to reach out through a healthy and practical model that is ours to use and benefit from.

First, Jesus did not deny His physical needs. He acknowledged those needs to Himself, choosing to rest and ask for water.

Second, Jesus did not put His physical needs before others' spiritual needs. He kept a healthy balance between the two, meeting His needs as well as those of others.

Third, Jesus did not try to hide His true self-identity. He willingly risked sharing that information even with His enemies.[9]

Summarizing Our Thoughts on Jesus and Feeling Thirsty and Weary

"So what?" So what that Jesus Christ felt weary and thirsty while moving through life? In what practical ways can this help you? Like Jesus, do not deny your physical needs. Acknowledge them to yourself and choose to meet them with honor like Jesus did. Like Jesus, do not put your physical needs before others' spiritual needs. Keep a healthy balance between the two, meeting your needs as well as those of others. Like Jesus, don't try to hide your true spiritual self-identity. Willingly risk sharing that information with others, even your enemies when the opportunity comes. As you discover and connect with Jesus' responses, He will satisfy both your spiritual and physical needs. Next, we read "one final word" about connecting with Jesus' emotions.

One Final Word

When Jesus walked and moved through life, He modeled more than 30 healthy, appropriate emotions which He expressed to the fullest extent. Diverse as His emotions are, they neither override nor disqualify each other. He went from compassion to indignation; depression to rejoicing; grief to gladness; joy to sorrow; love to anger; sympathy to feeling forsaken; weary thirst to hunger; and fear to peace. We can walk through the diversities of life like Jesus did when we discover and connect with His emotions and draw from His power, knowing that He understands what we are going through.[1] Until we are willing to grapple with Christ's diverse emotions, our ability to understand the process of human change will remain frustrated. We must clearly "see" the **whole** Christ, the God-man, who *felt* like we do; yet, whose emotions were of much greater quality than ours.

Christ's perfect personality comes from a balanced mental, physical, spiritual, and emotional wholeness. This "whole Christ" is who we're to model, imitate, and internalize within. For a mental balance we're to take on the "mind of Christ." For a physical balance we're to respectfully care for our body as a "temple of the Holy Spirit." For a spiritual balance we're to "become conformed to the image of Christ." For an emotional balance we're to "connect with the emotions of Jesus."[2] All four areas interact with each other. We cannot neglect even one, if we want to live healthy, productive, and balanced lives. Jesus has shown healthy emotions and how to live with them. Those who want to experience **whole** emotions rather than *toxic* emotions must begin to discover and connect with Jesus Christ's emotions. If you have not already done so, Jane and I hope and pray you will take the challenge.

Endnotes

Chapter One

1. Christoph Ernst Luthardt, "Was Jesus Really God and Man?" DECISION, Vol. 36, No. 12, December 1995, 27.

2. I have confirmed through various Scriptures that Jesus Christ felt and expressed in excess of 30 different emotions. All His emotional expressions were appropriate for the occasion and were displayed in a healthy, balanced manner. See index of the Emotions of Jesus in front of this book for a Scriptural basis of Christ's emotions.

3. B.B. Warfield, *The Person and Work of Christ* (Philadelphia, PA: Presbyterian and Reformed Publishing Company, 1950), 142, provided a basis for some of the ideas.

4. The basic idea for this emotions definition comes from Carroll E. Izard, *Human Emotions* (New York: Plenum Press, 1977), 3, 10, 18, 41.

5. Warfield, 124.

Chapter Two

1. Paraphrased story based on John 14:20-26.

2. Merrill C. Tenney, *John: The Gospel of Belief* (Grand Rapids, MI: Wm. B. Eerdmans Publishing Company, 1948), 225.

3. Joseph Henry Thayer, *A Greek-English Lexicon of the New Testament* (New York: American Book Company, 1889), 182; the definition for peace, *eirene*, is used of Jesus in John 14:27 and provides some basic thoughts.

4. Arthur W. Pink, *Gleanings From Paul* (Chicago, IL: Moody Press, 1967), 45.

5. R.V.G. Tasker, *The Epistle of Paul to the Romans* (Wm. B. Eerdmans Publishing Company, 1963), 120.

6. G. Campbell Morgan, *An Exposition of the Whole Bible* (Westwood, NJ: Fleming H. Revell Company, 1959), 447, and see Second Thessalonians 3:16, Lord of peace, and Hebrews 7:2, King of peace.

7. Christ's pattern for peace is based on (first) John 14:27; Romans 5:1; and Ephesians 2:8-9; (second) John 16:33; Mark 9:50; and Ephesians 2:13-14; (third) John 20:19,21,26; First Corinthians 7:15b; and Colossians 3:15 AMP.

Chapter Three

1. Kenneth S. Wuest, *Hebrews in the Greek New Testament* (Grand Rapids, MI: Wm. B. Eerdmans Publishing Company, 1956), 100; and 90-99 for some basic ideas.

2. Paraphrased story based on Hebrews 5:1-7.

3. Joseph Henry Thayer, *A Greek-English Lexicon of the New Testament* (New York: American Book Company, 1889), 259; definition for fear, *eulabeia*, used of Jesus in Hebrews 5:7.

4. From *Against the Night*, 10-11. Copyright © 1989 by Charles Colson. Published by Servant Publications, Box 8617, Ann Arbor, Michigan, 48107. Used by permission.

5. Thayer, 127; definition for timidity, *deilia*.

6. Ibid., 656; definition for terror, *phobos*.

7. Achlophobia, fear of crowds; acrophobia, fear of heights; agoraphobia, fear of open spaces; ailurophobia, fear of cats; anthophobia, fear of flowers; aquaphobia, fear of water; arachnophobia, fear of spiders; astraphobia, fear of lightning; brontophobia, fear of thunder; claustrophobia, fear of closed places; cynophobia, fear of dogs; demen tophobia, fear of insanity; equinophobia, fear of horses; herpephobia, fear of snakes; herpetophobia, fear of lizards, reptiles; mikrophobia, fear of germs; murophobia, fear of mice; mysophobia, fear of dirt, germs, contamination; numerophobia, fear of numbers; nyctophobia, fear of darkness; pyrophobia, fear of fire; thanatophobia, fear of death; trichophobia, fear of hair; xwnophobia, fear of strangers; zoophobia, fear of animals.

8. Thayer, 258; definition for reverential, godly fear, *eulabeia*, used in Hebrews 5:7.

9. James Montgomery Boice, *Foundations of the Christian Faith* (Downers Grove, IL: InterVarsity Press, 1986), 531.

10. C.S. Lewis, *The Screwtape Letters* (New York, NY: Bantam Books, 1982), viii.

11. William R. Newell, *Hebrews, Verse by Verse* (Chicago, IL: Moody Press, 1947), 161, provided some basic thoughts.

12. Christ's model of dealing with healthy fear is based on Hebrews 5:1-11.

Chapter Four

1. Paraphrased story based on Luke 8:40-48.

2. Joseph Henry Thayer, *A Greek-English Lexicon of the New Testament* (New York: American Book Company, 1889), 61; *The Analytical Greek Lexicon* (London: S. Bagster and Sons Limited), 42,195; Frederick W. Danker and F. Wilbur Gingrich, *A Greek-English Lexicon of the New Testament* (Chicago, IL: The University of Chicago Press, 1979), 789; and Robert L. Thomas, *New American Standard Exhaustive Concordance of the Bible* (Nashville, TN: Holman, 1981), 1634; definition for pressure of being squeezed, *apothlibo*; used of Jesus in Luke 8:45.

3. Alfred Marshall, *NASB-NIV Parallel New Testament in Greek and English* (Grand Rapids, MI: Zondervan Pub. House, 1986), 215; Bagster, 389; Thayer, 604; and Berry, *The Interlinear Literal Translation of the Greek New Testament* (Chicago, IL: Wilcox & Follet Company, 1952), 197; definition for pressure, *sunekomai*; as used of Jesus in Luke 12:50.

4. From my study of "pressure" and its five-word family, I found them used in the New Testament 68 times. Of these five Greek words Jesus felt two: the stress of <u>pressure</u>, *sunekomai*, and <u>squeeze</u>, *apothlibo*. The three words not used of Jesus are <u>pressure</u>, *thlibo*; <u>pressing together</u>, *thlispis*; and <u>anxiety</u>, *merimnate*. See Thayer, 61, 291, 604; Bagster, 42, 195, 389; Danker and Gingrich, 789; and Thomas, 1634.

5. From *You Can Profit From Stress* by Gary Collins, 13. Copyright 1977. Regal Books, Ventura, CA 93003. Used by permission.

6. Marshall, 215; Bagster, 389; Thayer, 604. Most authors translate *sunekomai* or its root word *suneko* as distressed, constrained, or straitened. However, Marshall says, "how am I **pressed**." Bagster says, "to be in a state of mental constriction, to be **hard pressed** by urgency of circumstances." Thayer says, "I am **hard pressed** on both sides, my mind is impelled or disturbed from each side." The "pressed" and "hard pressed" from the above authors mean "pressure" for Luke 12:50.

7. Christ's model of dealing with pressure is based on Luke 12:22-50.

Chapter Five

1. Paraphrased story based on Luke 22:39-46.

2. Joseph Henry Thayer, *A Greek-English Lexicon of the New Testament* (New York: American Book Company, 1889), 10; and *Wycliffe Bible Encyclopedia* (Chicago, IL: Moody Press, 1975), 31; definition for agony, *agonia*; used of Jesus in Luke 22:44.

3. From *You Can Profit From Stress* by Gary Collins, 13. Copyright 1977. Regal Books, Ventura, CA 93003. Used by permission.

4. Ibid., 13. Used by permission.

5. Warren Wiersbe, *God Isn't in a Hurry* (Grand Rapids, MI: Baker Books, 1994), 123.

6. Thayer, 10. The three Greek words in the "agony family" are *Agonia*, severe mental struggles and emotions; *Agonizonai*: contend with adversaries, endeavor or struggle with strenuous zeal; and *agon*, a contest of athletes and intense anxiety. Together they are used 14 times.

7. For more study on the four times Paul experienced the agony of intense anxiety, see Philippians 1:30; First Thessalonians 2:3; First Timothy 6:12; and Second Timothy 4:7.

8. Thayer, 10; agony, *agonizonai*, contend with adversaries, struggle with strenuous zeal.

9. Rosemead School of Psychology was started in 1970 by Dick Mohline, Bruce and Clyde Narramore, plus several faculty and staff members in Rosemead, California. Rosemead became one of the four schools of Biola University in LaMirada, California, in 1977. The first Christian school of psychology to receive APA approval, Rosemead now has over 500 graduates practicing in 45 states.

10. For one example of the wear and tear of living for Jesus, see Luke 22:44 for agony, *agonia*.

11. Christ's model of dealing with agony is based on Luke 22:39-46.

Chapter Six

1. Frederic W. Farrar, *The Life of Christ* (Minneapolis, MN: Klock & Klock Christian Publishers, Inc., 1982), 421.

2. Paraphrased story based on Matthew 27:11-26.

3. Frederick W. Danker and F. Wilbur Gingrich, *A Greek-English Lexicon of the New Testament* (Chicago, IL: The University of Chicago Press, 1979), 634; definition for suffering, *pascho*, used of Christ in First Peter 2:21.

4. Archibald D. Hart, *Adrenalin & Stress* (Waco, TX: Word Books Publisher, 1986), 20, 107, 117 provided some basic ideas.

5. Corrie ten Boom, *Clippings From My Notebook* (Minneapolis, MN: World Wide Publications, 1982), 51.

6. For study on Christ coming to our aid in our suffering, see Second Corinthians 1:5; Philippians 1:29; Second Timothy 1:12; Hebrews 2:18; and First Peter 1:20; 2:19; 3:17; 4:16,19.

7. For study on Christ suffering for us, see Matthew 16:21; Mark 8:31; 9:12; Luke 9:22; 22:15; 24:26; Acts 3:18; 17:3; Hebrews 5:8; 9:26; 12:13-14; and First Peter 1:21-25; 2:23-24; 3:18; 4:1.

8. P.B. Fitzwater, *Preaching and Teaching the New Testament* (Chicago, IL: Moody Press, 1957), 561.

9. Charles John Ellicott, *Ellicotts' Bible Commentary* (Grand Rapids, MI: Zondervan Publishing House, 1971), 1169.

10. Christ's model of dealing with stress is based on First Peter 2:18-24.

Chapter Seven

1. G. Campbell Morgan, *An Exposition of the Whole Bible* (Westwood, NJ: Fleming H. Revell Company, 1959), 425.

2. Paraphrased story based on Mark 2:23-28 and Mark 3:1-5.

3. Joseph Henry Thayer, *A Greek-English Lexicon of the New Testament* (New York: American Book Company, 1889), 595; and *The Analytical Greek Lexicon* (London: S. Bagster and Sons Limited), 382; definition for grieved, *sullupeomai*, used of Jesus in Mark 3:5.

4. Florence Littauer, *How to Get Along With Difficult People* (Eugene, OR: Harvest House Publishers, 1984), 8-9.

5. Lloyd J. Ogilvie, *Making Stress Work for You* (Waco, TX: Word Books Publisher, 1985), 37, 122; and Romans 7:15-16.

6. Arnold Burron and Jerry Crews, *Guaranteed Steps to Managing Stress* (Wheaton, IL: Tyndale House Publishers, Inc., 1986), 15,19.

7. While "Marsha" is not her name, this is our daughter and we love her dearly. You will read more about the sufferings from satanic ritual abuse (SRA) in endnote #5 of Chapter Twenty-five. Jane and I are very grateful for the way each of our children are allowing God to bring emotional and spiritual recovery and restoration into their lives.

8. Becki Conway Sanders, Jim & Sally Conway, *What God Gives When Life Takes* (Downers Grove, IL: InterVarsity Press, 1989), 85.

9. Ibid., 91.

10. Christ's model of dealing with the stress of grief is based on Mark 3:5.

Chapter Eight

1. Paraphrased story based on Matthew 8:1-4; 14:1-14.

2. Joseph Henry Thayer, *A Greek-English Lexicon of the New Testament* (New York: American Book Company, 1889), 584; definition for compassion, *splanknizomai*, used of Christ in Matthew 9:36. Some Greek

lexicons define compassion "to be moved as to one's bowels" since "the bowels were thought to be the seat of love and pity."

3. James Montgomery Boice, *Foundations of the Christian Faith* (Downers Grove, IL: InterVarsity Press, 1986), 282.

4. *Eleeo* (to show kindness, mildness): Jude 22; Mt. 18:33; Mk. 5:19; *matriopatheo* (display moderation): Heb. 5:2; *oikteiro* (to have pity or mercy): Rom. 9:15; *sumpatheo* (to suffer with another): Heb. 4:15; 10:34; 1 Pet. 3:8. These four Greek words combined with *splagnizomai* make up the compassion family. **Figurative usage** (1) of heart: Lk. 1:78; 2 Cor. 6:12; 7:15; Col. 3:12; Philem. 7,12,20. (2) of deeply felt affection, tender mercies: Phil. 1:8; 2:1. (3) Used of Jesus: Mt. 9:36; 14:14; 15:32; 18:27; 20:34; Mk. 1:41; 6:34; 9:22; Lk. 7:13; 10:33; 15:20.

5. Eleanor kept contact with close friends and family members during her two and one-half years of moving through the breast cancer experience. They ministered to her in loving care, compassion, patience, love, and God's guidance. I felt privileged to be a small part of her life in giving encouragement and counsel.

6. Robert Law, *The Emotions of Jesus* (New York, NY: Charles Scribner's Sons, 1915), 73.

7. Christ's model of feeling and showing compassion is based on Matthew 9:25-38.

Chapter Nine

1. Paraphrased story based on Matthew 11:19; 12:22-29; and Hebrews 3:1-8; 4:14-16.

2. Robert L. Thomas, *New American Standard Exhaustive Concordance of the Bible* (Nashville, TN: Holman, 1981), 1684; and Joseph Henry Thayer, *A Greek-English Lexicon of the New Testament* (New York: American Book Company, 1889), 596; definition for sympathy, *sumpatheo*, used of Jesus in Hebrews 4:15.

3. Thayer, 596; definition for another kind of sympathy, *sumpathas*, found in First Peter 3:8.

4. Ray C. Stedman, *Body Life* (Glendale, CA: Regal Books, 1979), 145-160.

5. Thomas C. Oden, *Life in the Spirit* (San Francisco, CA: Harper, 1992), 207.

6. Ibid., 57.

7. Thayer, 4; Frederick W. Danker and F. Wilbur Gingrich, *A Greek-English Lexicon of the New Testament* (Chicago, IL: The University of Chicago Press, 1979), 438; and Louis Berkof, *Systematic Theology*

(Grand Rapids, MI: Wm. B. Eerdmans Publishing Company, 1941), 455-56, provide the basis for the descriptions of *agape*, *koinonia*, and *ekklesia*.

8. A few groups to begin in churches: *Overcomers Outreach*, 2290 West Whittier Blvd., Suite D, La Habra, CA 90631, (310) 697-3994; a Christian ministry addressing alcoholism and drug dependency. *Sexaholics Anonymous* (SA), P.O. Box, Simi Valley, CA 93062; a Christian ministry sharing experiences, strength, and hope to help solve a common problem helping others to recover. *Childcare USA*, (800) 4-A-CHILD encourages us to become involved in working toward child abuse prevention. *Homosexuals Anonymous* (HA), HA Fellowship, P.O. Box 7881, Reading, PA 19603, began by two committed Christians to help those seeking freedom from homosexuality.

9. Using sympathy in restoring one another: Besides the practical and workable model Jesus gave us for showing sympathy, He designed a helpful and healthy way to restore a Brother or Sister in Galatians 6:1 by sympathizing with them in their weaknesses like Christ does with us.

First, establish a precedent of enduring with and carrying one another's burdens and troublesome moral faults (see Gal. 6:2). Paul does not suggest a codependency relationship, rather the opposite. (a) We're to realize that *sin is sin*, regardless of the type or label. (b) We're to *feel with* the fallen Christian and not relate with a pretended-sinless superiority, as though we've never sinned. This carrying another's burdens and faults suggests a need for respect and privacy. The fallen one's "sin information" should not be broadcast to the church or community or media.

Second, establish Scriptural instruction for them in gentleness, not harshness, or judging or accusing. This calls for hearing the facts without being critical or interrupting, except for fact-clarification questions. Listening gives the fallen Christian opportunity to state facts according to his/her perception. It shows what we're faced with.

Third, if possible, set a time frame for the restoration designed to reinstate the fallen one as a valued, forgiven Brother or Sister in *agape*-loving acceptance. Since each of us responds to counselling on a different time frame, individual needs must be upheld. Usually, the underlying reasons that cause most Christians to fall will span back to their childhood. These traumas, disappointments, violations, or broken trust must be dealt with for complete emotional and spiritual healing.

Fourth, design a "celebration time" where the restored Christian can share what God has done (see Gal. 6:6). This time can either be with the whole church body or a designated group that represents the local Church. The teacher(s) needs to accept the restored one as an equal spiritual peer. This frees one to move from restoring to a fully restored Brother or Sister. A special celebration time will also alert other members that sin is sin and must be dealt with. It demonstrates that restoring and reinstating are done in an absence of superiority. Jesus Christ gave this restoring-reinstating model for us, His Body, to use. On the whole, we have failed to do so and "shame" rests on us. In order for the *whole* Body of Christ to become restored, well, and shameless, we must use this Christ-designed way of showing sympathy to others going through trial.

    10. Neal Anderson with Joanne Anderson, *Daily in Christ: A Devotional* (Eugene, OR: Harvest House Publishers, 1993), May 2.

    11. Christ's model of feeling sympathy is based on Hebrews 4:12-16.

Chapter Ten

    1. Paraphrased story based on John 19:28-40 and Matthew 27:45-61.

    2. Kenneth W. Wuest, "Four Greek Words for Love" *Bibliotheca Sacra*, Vol. 116, No. 463, July-September 1959, 241-243; and Kenneth W. Wuest, *Bypaths in the Greek New Testament* (Grand Rapids, MI: Wm. B. Eerdmans Publishing Co., 1945), 117; definition for *agape* (love) used of Jesus in John 15:9,12.

    3. B.B. Warfield, *The Person and Work of Christ* (Philadelphia, PA: Presbyterian and Reformed Publishing Company, 1950), 104.

    4. Warfield, 101.

    5. Wuest, 111.

    6. C.S. Lewis, *The Four Loves* (New York, NY: Harcourt, Brace, and Company, 1960), 113.

    7. Wuest, *Bypaths*, 114.

    8. Wuest, *Bibliotheca Sacra*, 243.

    9. Christ's model in expressing *agape* (love) is based on John 15:8-10, chapters 12-17.

Chapter Eleven

    1. Paraphrased story based on John 11:17-44.

    2. Kenneth W. Wuest, "Four Greek Words for Love" *Bibliotheca Sacra*, Vol. 116, No. 463, July-September, 1959, 243; and Kenneth W. Wuest, *Bypaths in the Greek New Testament* (Grand Rapids, MI: Wm. B. Eerdmans Publishing Co., 1945), 122; definition for *phileo* (love) used of Jesus in John 15:9,12.

3. Many states are pushing for legislation that will protect them from the onslaught of same-sex marriage, if this abomination to God should be passed into federal law in this country. See *Family Policy*, a publication of the Family Research Council, Vol. 9, No. 1, February 1996, and *Family Voice*, Concerned Women for America, Vol. 18, No. 4, April 1996.

4. Wuest, 110.

5. Ibid., 110.

6. *Promise Keepers: Men of Integrity*, Promise Keepers booklet, Code 103, p. 12.

7. *Break Down the Walls*, Promise Keepers Men's Conference Program, 1996, p. 6.

8. Wuest, *Bibliotheca Sacra*, 242.

9. Wuest, *Bypaths*, 119.

10. Christ's model in expressing *phileo* (love) is based on John 11:1-36.

Chapter Twelve

1. James Strong, *Strong's Exhaustive Concordance of the Bible* (Nashville, TN: Manna Publishers), Dictionary of the Greek Testament, 77: definition for joy, *chara*, used of Jesus in John 15:11.

2. Paraphrased story based on John 15:1-11.

3. The Greeks used nine words for joy, to our one. **1)** *agalliasei* and **2)** *agalliao* (leap for joy, rejoice) Lk. 1:44; 1 Pet. 4:13; Jude 24-25: Joseph Henry Thayer, *A Greek-English Lexicon of the New Testament* (New York: American Book Company, 1889), 3; Alfred Marshall, *NASB-NIV Parallel New Testament in Greek and English* (Grand Rapids, MI: Zondervan Pub. House, 1986), 674. **3)** *kauchaomai* (glory, exult) Rom. 5:11: Marshall, 226. **4)** *euphrosune* (rejoicing or gladness) Acts 2:28; 14:17: *The Analytical Greek Lexicon* (London: S. Bagster and Sons Limited), 177. **5)** *skirtao* (leap for joy) Lk. 1:44; 6:23: Horst Balz and Gerhard Schneider, *Exegetical Dictionary of the New Testament* (Grand Rapids, MI: William B. Eerdmans Publishing Company, 1993), 254. **6)** *oninemi* (to have joy of) Philem. 20: Bagster, 289. **7)** *chara* (joy, gladness) Mt. 2:10, 13:20,44; Lk. 2:10; Jn. 15:11; 17:13; Phil. 2:2, 4:1: Marshall, 4, 40, 42, 166, 316, 322, 577. **8)** *charis* (favor, grace) Lk. 2:40; Acts 4:33; 7:46; 1 Pet. 2:19-20; Philem. 3,25: Thayer, 666, and Marshall, 168, 351, 362, 624, 625, 670. **9)** *chairo* (be glad, rejoice) Lk. 15:5; Jn. 4:36; 8:56; 11:35;

Acts 5:41; 8:39; 2 Cor. 7:7,13; Phil. 2:17; 1 Thess. 3:9: Thayer, 663, and Marshall, 222, 301, 531, 574, 592.

4. Charles Hodge, *Outlines of Discourses, Doctrinal and Practical* (New York, NY: Thomas Nelson and Sons, 1879), 280-281.

5. Ibid., 281.

6. B.B. Warfield, *The Person and Work of Christ* (Philadelphia, PA: Presbyterian and Reformed Publishing Company, 1950), 124-125.

7. Ibid., 126.

8. Robert Law, *The Emotions of Jesus* (New York, NY: Charles Scribner's Sons, 1915), 20.

9. Warfield, 126.

10. Warren W. Wiersbe, *Be Joyful* (Wheaton, IL: Victor Books, 1975), front of book as part of the subtitle.

11. Christ's model of feeling joy is based on John 15:1-11.

Chapter Thirteen

1. Alfred Edersheim, *The Life and Times of Jesus the Messiah*, Vol. II (New York, NY: Longmans, Green, and Company, 1899), 313, provides some basic thoughts.

2. Paraphrased story based on John 11:1-15.

3. Frederick W. Danker and F. Wilbur Gingrich, *A Greek-English Lexicon of the New Testament* (Chicago, IL: The University of Chicago Press, 1979), 873; James Strong, *Strong's Exhaustive Concordance of the Bible* (Nashville, TN: Manna Publishers), 77 of the Dictionary of the Greek Testament, and Horst Balz and Gerhard Schneider, *Exegetical Dictionary of the New Testament* (Grand Rapids, MI: William B. Eerdmans Publishing Company, 1993), 451; definition for glad, *chairo*, used of Jesus in John 11:14-15.

4. Jeri Krumroy, *Grief Is Not Forever* (Elgin, IL: Brethren Press, 1985), 68, 70.

5. Edersheim, 314.

6. Merrill F. Unger, *Unger's Bible Handbook* (Chicago, IL: Moody Press, 1966), 556.

7. Christ's model for feeling glad is based on John 11:1-16.

Chapter Fourteen

1. Paraphrased story based on Mark 5:1-20.

2. Mark I. Bubeck, *Overcoming the Adversary* (Chicago, IL: Moody Press, 1984), 34.

3. *The Analytical Greek Lexicon* (New York: NY: S. Bagster and Sons Limited, 1794), 2, 184; Alfred Marshall, *NASB-NIV Parallel New Testament in Greek and English* (Grand Rapids, MI: Zondervan Pub. House, 1986), 10; definition for rejoiced, *hagalliasato*, used of Jesus in Luke 10:21.

4. Andrew Murray, *With Christ in the School of Prayer* (Westwood, NJ: Fleming H. Revell Company, 1953), 145-146.

5. H.P. Liddon, "JOY— Our Crowning Gift," DECISION, Vol. 37, No. 4. April 1996, 27.

6. B.B. Warfield, *The Person and Work of Christ* (Philadelphia, PA: Presbyterian and Reformed Publishing Company, 1950), 123.

7. Christ's model of rejoicing is based on Luke 10:17-21.

Chapter Fifteen

1. Paraphrased story based on Matthew 26:20-35.

2. George Ricker Berry, *The Interlinear Literal Translation of the Greek New Testament* (Chicago, IL: Wilcox & Follett Company, 1952), 77. (Both Berry and Bagster translate *ademoneo* as depression); and *The Analytical Greek Lexicon* (London: S. Bagster and Sons Limited), 6; definition for depression, *adamoneo*, as used of Jesus in Matthew 26:37 Amplified.

3. DSM-IV^{TM}, *Diagnostic and Statistical Manual of Mental Disorders*, Fourth Edition (Washington, DC: The American Psychiatric Association, 1994), 327.

4. Archibald D. Hart, *Counseling the Depressed*, p. 11, Vol. 5 from *Resources for Christian Counseling* (Waco, TX: Word Books, 1987), Gary R. Collins, General Editor.

5. Ibid., 25-29.

6. Joseph Henry Thayer, *A Greek-English Lexicon of the New Testament* (New York: American Book Company, 1889), 11; Matthew 26:37.

7. Robert Plutchik, *The Emotions: Facts, Theories, and a New Model* (New York, NY: Random House, 1962), 55.

8. The 1979 suicide of Kenneth Nally is public knowledge. Ken's suicide is known because of the two trials held as a result of his father, Walter, suing Grace Community Church of Sun Valley, California, for clergy malpractice. Although I saw Ken one time, I was not named in the malpractice suit against Grace Community Church and its senior pastor, Dr. John McArthur. However, I was called on to testify at one of the trials.

9. Hart, 89. At least seven biological factors can be involved with biological caused depression. "They create conditions that could increase an individual's vulnerability to depression; reduce person's resistance to depression; set up 'deficits' in development that may make someone depression prone; increase vulnerability to stress induced depressions; shape the personality to be more depression prone; modify the functioning of the nervous system to create biochemical deficits or surpluses for depression; and slow down recovery mechanisms."

10. James F. Balch and Phyllis A. Balch, *Prescription for Nutritional Healing* (Garden City Park, NY: Avery Publishing Group Inc., 1990), 151-153.

11. Ibid., 27-31 and 151-153. Also Julian Whitaker, *Dr. Whitaker's Guide to Natural Healing* (Rocklin, CA: Prima Publishing, 1995), 100-105, 216-221.

12. Hart, 56-72.

13. Ibid., 87-99.

14. Ibid., 87-88.

15. Berry, 77.

16. Ibid., 419. Submission, *hupotassomenos*, a military term, means basically: To place oneself willingly under another's leadership. Even when the Holy Father asked Him to die for the sin of mankind, Christ placed Himself willingly under God's leadership.

17. Robert Law, *The Emotions of Jesus* (New York, NY: Charles Scribner's Sons, 1915), 133-134.

18. Christ's model of dealing with depression is based on Matthew 26:36-46.

Chapter Sixteen

1. Alfred Edersheim, *The Life and Times of Jesus the Messiah* (New York, NY: Longmans, Green, and Co., 1899), 593-613. According to an account from Temple times, the drape for the Most Holy Place entrance was 60 feet long, 30 feet wide, and the thickness of the palm of a hand sideways. The drape was worked together from 72 squares. It's estimated that 300 priests were required to manipulate the Temple drape. That's why we can confidently say the veil tearing was "really made by the Hand of God."

2. Paraphrased story based on Mark 15:34-36 and Matthew 27:45-54.

3. Joseph Henry Thayer, *A Greek-English Lexicon of the New Testament* (New York: American Book Company, 1889), 166; definition for forsaken, *engkataliepo*, used of Christ in Mark 15:34.

4. Robert Letham, *The Work of Christ* (Downers Grove, IL: Inter-Varsity Press, 1993), 172-173.

5. Everett F. Harrison, *A Short Life of Christ* (Grand Rapids, MI: Wm. B. Eerdmans Publishing Company, 1980), 223-224.

6. Edward John Carnell, *A Philosophy of the Christian Religion* (Grand Rapids, MI: Wm. B. Eerdmans Publishing Company, 1954), 383.

7. Ibid., 382.

8. Charles Hodge, *Outlines of Discourses, Doctrinal and Practical* (New York, NY: Thomas Nelson and Sons, Paternoster Row, 1879), 4.

9. For a broader study on God's sovereignty, see: Romans 8:28, things work together; Hebrews 13:5-8, trustworthy/never changing; Revelation 15:3-4, Leviticus 19:2, and Isaiah 6:3, Holy God; First Chronicles 29:11, head above all.

10. Charles Haddon Spurgeon, *The Treasury of the Bible*, Vol. 2 (Dunstable and London: Waterlow & Sons Limited, 1962), 440.

11. Ibid., 440.

12. Christ's model of dealing with feeling forsaken is based on Matthew 27:33-50 and Mark 15:22-34.

Chapter Seventeen

1. Paraphrased story based on John 12:27-36.

2. Joseph Henry Thayer, *A Greek-English Lexicon of the New Testament* (New York: American Book Company, 1889), 615; definition for troubled, *tarasso*, used of Christ in John 11:33.

3. B.B. Warfield, *The Person and Work of Christ* (Philadelphia, PA: Presbyterian and Reformed Publishing Company, 1950), 128-129.

4. James Montgomery Boice, *Foundations of the Christian Faith* (Downers Grove, IL: InterVarsity Press, 1986), 283.

5. Warfield, 129.

6. Charles Haddon Spurgeon, *The Treasury of the Bible*, Vol. 2 (Dunstable and London: Waterlow & Sons Limited, 1962), 440.

7. Jesus' model for dealing with feeling troubled is based on John 11:33-44.

Chapter Eighteen

1. Merrill C. Tenney, *John: The Gospel of Belief* (Grand Rapids, MI: Wm. B. Eerdmans Publishing Company, 1948), 172.

2. Some basic information was provided by Arthur W. Pink, *Exposition of the Gospel of John* (Grand Rapids, MI: Zondervan Publishing House, 1945), 238.

3. Paraphrased story based on Matthew 26:6-12; Mark 14:3-8; Luke 7:36-50; and John 12:1-8.

4. Robert Law, *The Emotions of Jesus* (New York, NY: Charles Scribner's Sons, 1915), 48.

5. Joseph Henry Thayer, *A Greek-English Lexicon of the New Testament* (New York: American Book Company, 1889), 359 and 124; definition for crying, *krauge*, and for tears, *dakruon*, both used of Jesus in Hebrews 5:7.

6. David W. Smith, *The Friendless American Male* (Ventura, CA: Regal Books, 1983), 17.

7. Ibid., Foreword.

8. B.B. Warfield, *The Person and Work of Christ* (Philadelphia, PA: Presbyterian and Reformed Publishing Company, 1950), 128-129.

9. Robert Law, *The Emotions of Jesus* (New York, NY: Charles Scribner's Sons, 1915), 49.

10. Christ's model for crying and shedding tears is based on Hebrews 5:1-10.

Chapter Nineteen

1. Paraphrased story based on Matthew 12:12-17; Mark 11:15-18; Luke 19:45-48; and John 2:14-17.

2. Joseph Henry Thayer, *A Greek-English Lexicon of the New Testament* (New York: American Book Company, 1889), 452; and W.E. Vine, *Expository Dictionary of New Testament Words* (Grand Rapids, MI: Zondervan Publishing House, 1952), 55-56; definition for anger, *orgee*, used of Christ in Mark 3:5.

3. Neil Clark Warren, *Make Anger Your Ally* (Garden City, NY: Doubleday & Company, Inc., 1983), 17.

4. Leslie S. Greenberg & Jeremy D. Safran, *Emotion in Psychotherapy* (New York, NY: The Guilford Press, n.d.), 173.

5. Warren, 18.

6. L. Jane Mohline, *A Woman of Excellence* (Nashville, TN: Broadman Press, 1991), 90.

7. Ibid., 90.

8. For a broader study on Christ's anger, see: Matthew 4:10; 21:12; Mark 3:5; 10:14; John 11:33,38; and Revelation 19:15

9. Christ's model of dealing with anger over other people's sin is based on Mark 3:1-6.

Chapter Twenty

1. Paraphrased story based on Matthew 18:1-10, Mark 10:13-16, and Luke 18:15-18.

2. *The Analytical Greek Lexicon* (London: S. Bagster and Sons Limited), 2; and Alfred Marshall, *NASB-NIV Parallel New Testament in Greek and English* (Grand Rapids, MI: Zondervan Publishing House, 1986), 133; definition for indignation, *aganakteo*, used of Jesus in Mark 10:14.

3. Dwight L. Carlson, *Overcoming Hurts & Anger* (Eugene, OR: Harvest House Publishers, 1981), 38-39.

4. Bitterness, *pikria*, is found in Matthew 26:75; Luke 22:62; Acts 8:23; Ephesians 4:31; Colossians 3:19; Hebrews 12:15; and Revelation 10:19. This emotion was not felt by Jesus Christ.

5. Exasperate, *parorgisimos*, is found in Romans 10:19; Ephesians 4:26; and 6:4. Some have wrongly translated exasperation as wrath. This emotion was not felt by Jesus Christ.

6. Edward John Carnell, *A Philosophy of the Christian Religion* (Grand Rapids, MI: Wm. B. Eerdmans Publishing Company, 1954), 438.

7. Ibid., 439.

8. Christ's model of dealing with indignation is based on Mark 10:13-16.

Chapter Twenty-one

1. Paraphrased story based on Matthew 23:16-34 and Mark 8:11-12.

2. Joseph Henry Thayer, *A Greek-English Lexicon of the New Testament* (New York: American Book Company, 1889), 42; definition for deep sighing, *anastenazo*, as used of Jesus in Mark 8:12.

3. Ibid., 42.

4. Christ's model of dealing with sighing deeply is based on Mark 8:11-13 and Matthew 16:1-4.

Chapter Twenty-two

1. Paraphrased story based on Revelation 19:11-16.

2. Joseph Henry Thayer, *A Greek-English Lexicon of the New Testament* (New York: American Book Company, 1889), 293; definition for fury, *thumos*, used of Jesus in Revelation 19:15.

3. "Frank" is not this young man's name, but I came to appreciate him and his growing, developing, and maturing love for the Lord.

4. Christ's model of feeling fury over other people's unrepented sin is based on Revelation 19:1-19.

5. Dwight L. Carlson, *Overcoming Hurts & Anger* (Eugene, OR: Harvest House Publishers, 1981), 47.

Chapter Twenty-three

1. Paraphrased story based on Mark 14:17-42.

2. Joseph Henry Thayer, *A Greek-English Lexicon of the New Testament* (New York: American Book Company, 1889), 195; and George Ricker Berry, *The Interlinear Literal Translation of the Greek New Testament* (Chicago, IL: Wilcox & Follett Company, 1952), 137; definition for amazement, *ekthambeo*, used of Christ in Mark 14:32-33.

3. Andrew Murray, *With Christ in the School of Prayer* (Westwood, NJ: Fleming H. Revell Company, 1953), 44-45.

4. Timothy M. Warner, *Spiritual Warfare* (Wheaton, IL: Crossway Books, 1991), 141.

5. For sound teaching on "warfare praying" read: Neil T. Anderson, *Victory Over the Darkness* and *The Bondage Breaker*; Mark I. Bubeck, *The Adversary* and *Overcoming the Adversary*; Kathy Casto, *How to Pray for Your Loved Ones* (Hisway Publications, P.O. Box 418, Rockwall, TX 75087); and Timothy M. Warner, *Spiritual Warfare*. Providing excellent teaching for putting on God's Armor is a tape set by Dr. David Jeremiah, *The Armor of the Believer* (Turning Point, P.O. Box 3838, San Diego, CA 92163).

6. Murray, 156.

7. Christ's model of dealing with life's dilemmas is based on Mark 14:32-42.

Chapter Twenty-four

1. Paraphrased story based on Matthew 8:5-13.

2. Joseph Henry Thayer, *A Greek-English Lexicon of the New Testament* (New York: American Book Company, 1889), 284; definition for marveled, *thamazo*, used of Jesus in Mark 6:6 and Matthew 8:10.

3. Carroll E. Izard, *Human Emotions* (New York, NY: Plenum Press, 1977), 6.

4. L. Jane Mohline, *A Woman of Excellence* (Nashville, TN: Broadman Press, 1991), 15.

5. Neil Anderson with Joanne Anderson, *Daily in Christ: A Devotional* (Eugene, OR: Harvest House Publishers, 1993), December 5.

6. Vernard Eller, *The Language of Canaan and the Grammar of Feminism* (Grand Rapids, MI: Wm. B. Eerdmans Publishing Company, 1982), 38.

7. Christ's model of dealing with marvel in dilemmas is based on Matthew 8:1-10 and Hebrews 12:1-3.

Chapter Twenty-five

1. Merrill F. Unger, *Unger's Bible Handbook* (Chicago, IL: Moody Press, 1966), 524; and R.V.G. Tasker, *The Gospel According to St. John* (Grand Rapids, MI: Wm. B. Eerdmans Publishing Company, 1965), 139.

2. Paraphrased story based on Luke 7:11-17 and John 11:30-37.

3. Joseph Henry Thayer, *A Greek-English Lexicon of the New Testament* (New York: American Book Company, 1889), 207; and Alfred Marshall, *NASB-NIV Parallel New Testament in Greek and English* (Grand Rapids, MI: Zondervan Publishing House, 1986), 1648; definition for deeply moved, *embrimaomai*, as used of Christ in John 11:33.

4. Robert Law, *The Emotions of Jesus* (New York, NY: Charles Scribner's Sons, 1915), 101.

5. While "Donald" is not his name, this is our eldest son. God is doing His healing work and restoration in him through Bible study, prayer, counseling, and encouragement from his wife and friends. He was forced to watch and be a part of heinous, demonic rituals in which babies or little children were brutally, sexually violated and then sacrificed on altars dedicated to satan. God continues to bring spiritual and emotional healing into his mind, emotions, spirit, and body. Our children's experiences are typical of stories from thousands plus thousands of SRA survivors who have never met. Although in any walk of life we will find successful liars counterfeiting the truth, it's **impossible** for these types of stories to keep surfacing across the country from persons who have never met unless the stories are true. Our adult children have *nothing to gain* by telling their accounts, but everything to lose.

6. Chuck Colson, Prison Fellowship Ministries monthly-support letter of October 24, 1989. See Charles Colson, *The God of Stones & Spiders* (Wheaton, IL: Crossway Books, 1990), 178-180.

7. Merrill C. Tenney, *John: The Gospel of Belief* (Grand Rapids, MI: Wm. B. Eerdmans Publishing Company, 1951), 174; and P.B. Fitzwater, *Preaching and Teaching the New Testament* (Chicago, IL: Moody Press, 1957), 306; both provided some basic thoughts.

8. Taken from *Ellicott's Bible Commentary* by Charles John Ellicott, 835. Copyright © 1971 by Zondervan Publishing House. Used by permission of Zondervan Publishing House.

9. Christ's model of dealing with feeling deeply moved is based on John 11:33-35.

Chapter Twenty-six

1. Paraphrased story based on Matthew 26:20-38.

2. P.B. Fitzwater, *Preaching and Teaching the New Testament* (Chicago, IL: Moody Press, 1957), 95; and Charles John Ellicott, *Ellicott's Bible Commentary* (Grand Rapids, MI: Zondervan Publishing House, 1971), 746; provide some basic thoughts.

3. Joseph Henry Thayer, *A Greek-English Lexicon of the New Testament* (New York: American Book Company, 1889), 50; and Horst Balz and Gerhard Schneider, *Exegetical Dictionary of the New Testament* (Grand Rapids, MI: William B. Eerdmans Publishing Company, 1993), 74; definition for sad, *perilupos*, used of Christ in Matthew 26:38.

4. Neil Anderson with Joanne Anderson, *Daily in Christ: A Devotional* (Eugene, OR: Harvest House, 1993), September 6; provided the basic thought about "looming" circumstances.

5. G. Campbell Morgan, *An Exposition of the Whole Bible* (Westwood, NJ: Fleming H. Revell Company, 1959), 421-422.

6. William Counts, "Jesus in the Garden of Gethsemane," *Psychology for Living*, Vol. XVIII, No. 4, April 1976, 8.

7. Ibid., 8.

8. Christ's model of dealing with sadness is based on Matthew 26:26-46.

Chapter Twenty-seven

1. Merrill C. Tenney, *John: The Gospel of Belief* (Grand Rapids, MI: Wm. B. Eerdmans Publishing Company, 1951) 200; provides some basic thoughts.

2. Charles John Ellicott, *Ellicott's Bible Commentary* (Grand Rapids, MI: Zondervan Publishing House, 1971), 746; Alfred Edersheim, *The Life and Times of Jesus the Messiah*, Vol. 2 (New York, NY: Longmans, Green, and Co., 1899), 533-41; and G. Campbell Morgan, *An Exposition of the Whole Bible* (Westwood, NJ: Fleming H. Revell Company, 1959), 421; provide some basic thoughts.

3. Paraphrased story based on Matthew 26:26-41.

4. James Strong, *Strong's Exhaustive Concordance* (Nashville, TN: Manna Publishers), 45, 959; and George V. Wigram, *The Englishman's Greek Concordance* (Grand Rapids, MI: Baker Book House, 1979) 465, 986; definition for sorrow, *lupeo*, used of Jesus in Matthew 26:38.

5. Joni Eareckson & Steve Estes, *A Step Further* (Grand Rapids, MI: Zondervan Publishing House, 1978), 15-24; Bob Dole's August 15, 1996, acceptance speech at the Republican Convention. After healing from war wounds, he spent 35 years serving in government.

6. B.B. Warfield, *The Person and Work of Christ* (Philadelphia, PA: Presbyterian and Reformed Publishing Company, 1950), 126-127.

7. Christ's model of dealing with sorrow is based on Matthew 26:26-46.

Chapter Twenty-eight

1. Alfred Edersheim, *The Life and Times of Jesus the Messiah* (New York, NY: Longmans, Green, and Co., 1899), 317.

2. Ibid., 320, 322; and B.B. Warfield, *The Person and Work of Christ* (Philadelphia, PA: Presbyterian and Reformed Publishing Company, 1950), 115-117; provide some basic thoughts.

3. Paraphrased story based on John 11:17-35.

4. Edersheim, 325.

5. Joseph Henry Thayer, *A Greek-English Lexicon of the New Testament* (New York: American Book Company, 1889), 124; and *The Analytical Greek Lexicon* (New York, NY: S. Bagster and Sons Limited, 1794), 84; definition for wept, *dakruo*, used of Jesus in John 11:35.

6. Although "Alan" is not his real name, this is a brief history of our youngest son. We are very grateful for his commitment to the Lord and emotional, spiritual growth. The following is his understanding and teaching about God's sovereignty. "It's normal for survivors to feel that even if God is sovereign He can't be loving and good because a good and loving God can't allow such awful pain and suffering. Yet, I've come to understand that God is 100% sovereign and 100% loving and good. Or better said, perfect in love, goodness, and sovereignty. I believe God wants His love to motivate us in each area of our lives, and wants our love. While love is our basis for relationship with God, I believe His sovereignty is one of the—and perhaps the most—important truths to understand for anyone, especially an abuse victim. It's the bottom-line issue for us to grapple with. For if God is not in ultimate control of all things, then it's possible we could be separated from His love, making that love of no effect to us. As well, if God is not in ultimate control then His promises are not absolute. Only a perfect and sovereign God can carry out His many plans and promises without fail."

Survivors of SRA (satanic ritual abuse) or other abuses have difficulty coming to a sound understanding of God's sovereignty in trying to deal with their memories and troubled souls. They cry out, "Where is God? Why doesn't He help me? Who is in control? God, why did You allow those evil people to take me? Why didn't You stop them? Why did You let them hurt me?" A troubled soul overshadows their lives as adults and they have difficulty trusting anyone, especially God. This explains why a good-sized portion of Christ's Body struggles with the trust, commitment, and submission needed in trying to deal with God's sovereignty and in coping with our damaged emotions.

7. Warfield, 116-117, 119.

8. Christ's model of weeping during times of loss is based on John 11:32-35.

Chapter Twenty-nine

1. Alfred Edersheim, *The Life and Times of Jesus the Messiah* (London and Bombay: Longmans, Green, and Company, 1899) Vol. I, 281-282, 300.

2. Paraphrased story based on Matthew 3:13-17 and Luke 4:1-2.

3. Edersheim, 281.

4. Joseph Henry Thayer, *A Greek-English Lexicon of the New Testament* (New York, NY: American Book Company, 1889), 498; and *The Analytical Greek Lexicon* (New York, NY: S. Bagster and Sons Limited, 1794), 314; definition of hunger, *peinao*, as used of Jesus in Matthew 4:2.

5. P.B. Fitzwater, *Preaching and Teaching the New Testament* (Chicago, IL: Moody Press, 1957), 28.

6. Charles John Ellicott, *Ellicott's Bible Commentary* (Grand Rapids, MI: Zondervan Publishing House, 1971), 688.

7. C. Fred Dickason, *Angels Elect & Evil* (Chicago, IL: Moody Press, 1995), 11.

8. Nancy Gibbs, "Angels Among Us," *Time*, December 27, 1993, 56.

9. Billy Graham, *Angels, God's Secret Agents* (Waco, TX: Word Books, 1986), 27.

10. Dickason, 25.

11. Ibid., 29-31.

12. Arkansas Baptist, Vol. 95, No. 20, October 3, 1996, 3.

13. Christ's model for dealing with hunger is based on Matthew 4:1-7.

Chapter Thirty

1. Charles John Ellicott, *Ellicott's Bible Commentary* (Grand Rapids, MI: Zondervan Publishing House, 1971), 813.

2. Arthur W. Pink, *Exposition of the Gospel of John* (Grand Rapids, MI: Zondervan Publishing House, 1974), 175, 177, 198; provided some basic ideas.

3. Paraphrased story based on John 4:5-26.

4. Joseph Henry Thayer, *A Greek-English Lexicon of the New Testament* (New York: American Book Company, 1889), 355; definition for weary, *kopiao*, used of Jesus in John 4:6; Thayer, 153; and Alfred Marshall, *NASB-NIV Parallel New Testament in Greek and English* (Grand Rapids, MI: Zondervan Publishing House, 1986), 330; definition for thirsty, *dipsao*, used of Jesus in John 19:28.

5. L. Jane Mohline, *A Woman of Excellence* (Nashville, TN: Broadman Press, 1991), 128.

6. Mohline, 149-150.

7. John Barclay, *The Gospel of John*, Vol. 2 (Philadelphia, PA: The Westminster Press, 1975), 258.

8. Pink, 162.

9. Christ's model of dealing with hunger and thirst is based on John 4:1-19.

One Final Word

1. James Montgomery Boice, *Foundations of the Christian Faith* (Downers Grove, IL: InterVarsity Press, 1986), 285.

2. To study the "four" balances, see: Luke 2:52; Romans 2:5; Second Corinthians 6:14-18; 3:18; Colossians 1:15.